zen and the ways

T0151427

Published by The Buddhist Society
Patron: His Holiness the Dalai Lama
Registered Charity No. 1113705

First published in 1978 by Routledge & Kegan Paul Ltd.,
London and Shambhala Publications, Inc., Boulder, Colorado
Second edition published by Charles E. Tuttle Publishing Co. 1987
Third edition published by The Buddhist Society 2017
© The Trevor Leggett Adhyatma Yoga Trust, 2017

Publication supported by The Trevor Leggett Adhyatma Yoga Trust.

ISBN: 978-0-901032-47-8 (The Buddhist Society)

A catalogue record for this book is available from the British
Library

Edited by Sarah Auld
Designed by Avni Patel

Printed in Padstow, Cornwall by TJ International

The Buddhist Society
58 Eccleston Square
London
SW1V 1PH
T: 020 7834 5858
E: info@thebuddhistsociety.org
thebuddhistsociety.org

zen and the ways

Trevor Leggett

To the late Dr Hari Prasad Shastri, one-time lecturer in Indian Philosophy to the University of Waseda and friend of Marquis Okuma, its founder, these translations and transcriptions from the Japanese are reverently dedicated.

Contents

Preface

Zen is practice and realisation of the Buddha heart. Its tradition came from India associated with extreme detachment, fearlessness and meditation. Its practice is inquiry into the nature of self. Its realisation is the transcendental aloneness of the Buddha's 'In heaven and earth I alone am the World-honoured one.' In expression it has shown freedom from fear of death, a certain carelessness as to what may happen, and inspiration in all the concerns of life, great and small.

Zen came from India to China in the sixth century, and from China to Japan in the thirteenth. In China the Zen master was still living in remote temples on mountains; in Japan Zen was adopted by the warrior government ruling from Kamakura, and many of the temples (though still called 'mountains') were near cities. The tradition developed that Zen could be practised in and through things like fencing, painting, flower arrangement, writing with a brush, serving tea and so on, and when so practised they were termed Ways.

This book has six parts: Zen; Kamakura Zen; The Kamakura Koans; The Ways; Texts of the Ways; Stories of the Ways; and there are three appendices.

Part One presents Zen mainly in the words of twentieth-century masters, especially the koan or riddle system which developed in China. In this section and in the others I have used mainly material which has not been translated before.

Part Two, Kamakura Zen, describes the warrior Zen of the first three hundred years in Japan. The main text is the classic 'On Meditation' by the master Daikaku, one of the founders of Zen in Japan.

The Kamakura koans are almost unknown even in Japan, and the text which is here translated in part is of extreme rarity and interest. A full account of it is given in the appendices.

In Part Four the Ways are presented from traditional sources, mostly the so-called 'secret scrolls' preserved in the schools of the Ways. In this section some explanations are given, based on the oral instruction which accompanied the scrolls.

Part Five gives extracts from the less cryptic parts of scrolls themselves.

Part Six gives some of the stories of the Ways in practice. A number of these I have never seen written anywhere. I heard them when these things were being discussed and, believing them worth preserving, I transcribe them here. Some have a number of variations.

The appendices, by F. Imai, a famous scholar of the 1920s, concern the text on the Kamakura koans called Shonankattoroku, and there is also an index of the Chinese characters of the names.

The Zen method of instruction is not systematic exposition. Zen teachers believe that realisation does not develop from ordinary thinking; in fact it is by its very nature to some extent opposed to it. So the method is by giving riddling stories and analogies, in the expectation that one or more of them will strike a spark. It is similar to instruction in an art, and quite different from instruction in a science. To a particular frame of mind this is merely irritating, in which case Zen will have nothing to give. The method involves a high failure rate among pupils, but it produces remarkable successes also.

In this book names, both Japanese and Chinese, are given as the Japanese pronounce them. No diacritical marks are used; the important words and names in Zen will no doubt become anglicised, as judo and kendo have been. The family name comes first, and then the personal name. For the benefit of historians, I have included at the end an index of the characters with which the less well-known names referred to in Imai's comments are written. Some of the readings are unusual and not to be found in present-day dictionaries; I have however followed Imai on the assumption that these were Kamakura readings verified by him.

Acknowledgements

Some of the translations here have already appeared in *The Young East* published by Tohokai, Tokyo, and *Self-Knowledge* published by Shanti Sadan, London, to whom I am grateful for permission to reproduce them.

For permission to use the picture of the Nelson Column, my thanks go to the artist Matsumoto Hozan and to the Japanese Service of the British Broadcasting Corporation, to which it was first presented, and for the two pictures of the mirror, to Morikawa Atsuko who presented these expressions of mirror Zen to this book.

Thanks for the photographs from his dojo to Omori Sogen Roshi, present head of Tesshu Society, Tokyo.

I am grateful to Professor Nakamura Hajime for so ingeniously locating what may be the only extant copy of Imai's original edition of Shonankattoroku, and to the priest of Kichijo temple who generously allowed it to be photographed. Professor Nakamura also kindly looked over the Appendices and supplied unusual readings.

Thanks to the Society for International Education, Tokyo, and to the British Museum, for the pictures accredited to them on the respective pages.

Finally I am grateful to Mr. Watanabe Kisaburo, 7th Dan, of the Budokan, Tokyo, for demonstrating the techniques on page 288 and for use of the Judo contest photograph from the Asian Games on page 246.

Part One

Zen

Zen is a Japanese word derived through a Chinese approximate pronunciation from the Buddhist hybrid Sanskrit 'dhyana', which means illumined trance. The word is written in Japanese with the Chinese character imported along with the concept.

Zen

The left-hand side of the character is what is called the radical, and gives the general class to which it belongs; this radical is associated with religion and with happiness. It is itself a character. It is

radical no. 113 radical no. 145 'alone'

similar to (and often confused with) another radical, which has the meaning 'garment'. The right-hand side gives a rough guide to the pronunciation, but this too is often chosen, out of several possible ones, for its appropriateness; here the right-hand side means 'alone'. It is a character in its own right.

Most Chinese characters have at least two pronunciations in Japan. One is an approximation to the way the Chinese pronounced them (in the sixth, eighth or fourteenth century depending on the circumstances), and the other is a native

Japanese word chosen to give the meaning of the character. 'Zen' is one of the few characters which has only one reading, the Chinese one. There was no Japanese word with the

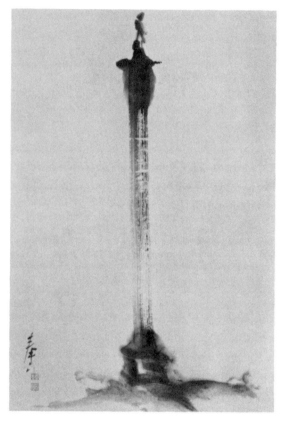

A Zen picture of a familiar scene. The artist has altered the proportions of column and figure to express the transcendental aloneness of Zen. (Matsumoto Hozan)

ZEN AND THE WAYS

meaning of transcendental aloneness contained in the structure of this Chinese character.

The warriors who trained in Zen when it first took root in Japan in the thirteenth century were sometimes uncertain about the exact make-up of the less common characters. Two of the stories which will come later turn on a mix-up between two very similar radicals, No. 115 and No. 145, the latter having one small stroke extra, and the meaning 'garment'.

When this is put to the right-hand side 'alone', the sense is a single cotton garment, generally an undergarment, and some warriors thought that Zen took its name from mountain ascetics wearing only one thin robe; others mistook both sides of the character, and supposed that Zen was written with a character whose meaning is 'loin-cloth'. These mistakes became the subject of koan riddles, and the teachers turned them to spiritual use.

'one-robe' 'loin-cloth'

Dhyana was only one of the methods of Buddhist practice, others being Morality and Insight. But the word Zen was extended to mean realisation of spiritual transcendence beyond all distinctions, and also expression of the transcendent within the world distinctions, illusory as they are. The reader who has no idea of Zen might now read the short 'Zazenron' classic by one of the masters who brought Zen to Japan (see p. 69).

The diagram below is not a diagram, but only an indication; the existence of the line itself is merely theoretical.

> Above that line, the absolute is actual
> and the world of distinctions only theoretical

THERE IS A LINE DRAWN IN EMPTY SPACE

> Below that line, the world of distinctions is actual
> and the absolute only theoretical

Books and words are concerned with the world of distinctions; Zen in the world of distinctions drives at realisation that the distinctions are only theoretical. Though theoretical, distinctions can express something, and the true expression of the universe is called Buddha-nature. Zen in the world of distinctions aims at realisation of the universal Buddha-nature, which is

clearly realised and clearly expressed by the Buddha-in-his-own-glory,

clearly realised but to an ordinary eye not so clearly expressed by the Buddha-engaged-in-activity,

little realised and little expressed by the ordinary being in his ordinary activity.

To the Buddha-eye, everything in the universe animate or inanimate is expressing in its changes the universal Buddha-nature; these are 'theoretical' changes of what is beyond definition as changing or not changing. Mental agitation, and especially the desire that things should not change, obscures the expression of Buddha-nature.

Transcendence is beyond words.

In the world of distinctions, there are the two aspects: Buddha-realisation, and Buddha-action. Buddha-realisation is awareness of the harmony in the cosmic current of change; Buddha-action expresses inspiration arising from awareness of that harmony.

Buddha-realisation must be recognition of Buddha-life in the tiniest things. Just as when one knows someone very well, one can recognise him at a distance, or from a passing glimpse in a crowd, or from his hand-writing or voice, so the Zen man has to be able to recognise the Buddha in everything. Many of the classical meditations are concerned with developing this power of recognition, and are therefore presented in the form of a riddle, technically called 'koan'.

As to what that recognition experience might be like, there is this illustration. A man in a big department store sees someone in the distance approaching and looking at him with interest. He cannot quite place who it is, though there is something familiar. Coming closer, he finds it is himself reflected in a large mirror. Then he smiles. Even an experienced Zen man may have his awareness momentarily clouded over sometimes, but he awakens almost at once, and when he does, he smiles. There is a hint in this little incident which is often not grasped for some time, though many people think the meaning is 'obvious'.

Koan Zen

The principle of the koan (literally an official declaration) is something like English case-law, or collating scientific observations: a principle is extracted from concrete individual cases. In theory anything, if investigated to the limit, reveals Buddha-nature, and not merely theoretically but practically. But most ordinary things do not have enough 'charge' of feeling to hold attention for very long, and in many cases the principle is difficult to observe because it is masked by the circumstances. If one wants to discover, or confirm, the effect of gravity, one should not choose as his field of experiment and observation the fall of a feather. Gravity is as fully operative there as anywhere, but the influence of air resistance, wind and so on obscure its working. Advanced students do indeed tackle just such problems, but they are not appropriate when establishing the basic principle.

In any life which is controlled and where an inquiry into truth is being pursued with the help of meditation practice, a koan develops of itself. 'Why do Buddhas go around teaching when the Buddha-nature is in all living beings?' was a koan which arose in the mind of the young Dogen. But it often takes many years (thirty years in one tradition) before a man can identify, then formulate and then resolve the point which has worried him all his life. Many of these spontaneous crystallizations of the life-problem are recorded in biographies of Zen masters of the Tang dynasty; later on in China one of them would sometimes be set to a student as a centre round which his own problem could crystallise more quickly. They were then called koans. They mostly cut across ordinary assumptions about the world and the self, and often about Buddhist doctrine as well.

One of the most famous concerns a question about a dog. The story first appears as a koan in the Shoyoroku collection. A monk asked Master Joshu, 'Is there Buddha-nature in a dog or not?'

Joshu said, 'There is.'

The monk said, 'How should it be shut up in a bag of bones?'

Then on another occasion a monk asked Joshu, 'Is there Buddha-nature in a dog or not?'

And Joshu answered, 'Not'.

The monk said, 'Buddha-nature is in all – how should it not be in a dog?'

In the somewhat later collection called Mumonkan only the second question-and-answer appears, and this is the usual form of the koan. As the monk says, it is on the face of it opposed to Buddhist doctrine.

To salvage the answer philosophically is not too diffi-cult. Some say that the Buddha-nature being everywhere, and reality, it is only by illusion that individual things are discerned in it. The question postulates the dog as a real entity, and wonders whether there is Buddha-nature in it or not. But the true question is whether there is any entity to be called 'dog' in all-pervading Buddha-nature. So Joshu answered 'Not' in order to reject the whole basis of the monk's original question.

Others say that Buddha-nature is not in the dog, but the dog is Buddha-nature from nose to tail-tip, so again the Not is to reject the basis of the question.

Such intellectually agile answers have little value in Zen and are no help in life. While the question is purely theoretical, its solution has no more urgency than a crossword. It is not a koan. The time may come however when the inquirer confronts directly great temptation or great fear; then he is the dog and really needs to know 'Is there Buddha-nature in the dog or not?' Joshu's answer is not a facile one, and everything has to be thrown in to the effort to solve it – will, emotions, thinking and life itself. An answer has to come out with the unanimous and vigorous assent of every element in the individual. An intellectual answer, for instance, is useless if the real feeling and behaviour do not accord with it; similarly useless is a state of emotional excitement screwed up to blanket hidden doubts.

Westerners (and Japanese too) sometimes get the idea that the main thing is a sort of cheek; anything unusual done with an appearance of complete confidence would be accepted. There are jokes about a Zen man asking for a night's lodging, and tested with a koan at the gate; not knowing the proper answer, he brashly hits the gate hard with his wooden clog. The gate-keeper passes him in, and it later turns out that he did not know the answer either, but assumed that it must be to hit the gate with a clog.

This sort of thing happens in the world everywhere, not only in Zen. Foreigners studying Japanese often brag about the number of written characters they have learned. A long time ago I knew an Irishman in Tokyo who enjoyed deflating these pretensions, by suddenly demanding, 'Write the character *utsu*, melancholy.' This was famous as one of the most difficult characters, with twenty-nine strokes (it has now been simplified), and nearly every student had seen it some time as a curiosity. With many hesitations and corrections, the victim would produce a version; the Irishman would glance at it and say 'Wrong!', watching with amusement as the other pored over his version with a chastened air. But one day I saw him challenge a Belgian, who unexpectedly dashed off the character immediately on a piece of paper and handed it across; the Irishman scrutinised it and then admitted that it was right. I picked up the piece of paper, and afterwards checked it against a dictionary, finding to my surprise that there were two mistakes. I pointed these out to the Irishman and asked, 'Why did you pass it?'

He replied, 'How should I know how to write it? I always say it's wrong and they accept that. But when he wrote it so confidently I thought it must be right.'

'utsu' (melancholy)

When there is mutual ignorance, confidence indeed is king.

A koan answer has to be something living, not parroted. There are answers which contradict themselves. A Chinese clerk applying for a job with an English company in Hong Kong was asked whether he knew English grammar. He replied enthusiastically, 'Me English grammar number one expert. Top-side!

In a high-grade judo examination sometimes questions are asked; one of them can be 'What is shizentai posture?'

To answer this the man could say, 'Upright and relaxed, feet about twelve inches apart, centre of gravity midway between feet.' As he answered, he would have to be in that posture. It is quite difficult to demonstrate a good shizen-tai, and this is the point of the question. Verbally it could be answered in more detail and more correctly, by saying that the distance between the little toes should be the same as the distance between the outside of the shoulders, and the centre of gravity should be above the mid-point of the line between the little toes. But in judging the answer, the examiners would look to see whether in fact the examinee's little toes were that distance apart, and whether the distribution of weight was what was being described. If not, the answer would not be accepted. An expert might stand without a word, demonstrating a splendid shizentai posture. He would get full marks.

A modern Zen master, who is a devotee of Amida, remarks that his pupils know it, and sometimes come into his interview room saying the mantra of Amida with great reverence: Namu Amida Butsu. But he never passes this answer. 'It's like little girls talking about married life, or Boy Scouts talking about war. Often they are repeating what they have heard or read and it is quite sensible, but the fact is that they know nothing about it.'

In the judo examination, the man has to assume and demonstrate in himself the posture which he is describing, and in Zen it is the same. If fearlessness is to be expressed, the man has to be fearless; if it is devotion, it has to be real devotion, and not trying out on the teacher an appearance of devotion.

All the koans drive at a reality in the universe and in the individual, partly but not wholly obscured by eddies in the stream of thought. In early Zen it was held that to pass through one is to pass through all. When concentration on one is complete, the thoughtstreams suddenly stop and the koan is transcended. Afterwards thought is taken up again, but without eddies in the stream. The realisation is expressed in relative terms as power and as compassion, especially in creation of beauty. Traditionally an expression of realisation may take the form of a verse, but in any case it is usual that the first expression has a relation to the theme of the koan by means of which it came about.

The koan is a theme to catch the mind. It must matter to a man who wants to take it up, and a teacher selects an appropriate one to suit the type of pupil before him. (The conviction of most pupils that they are unique is nearly always a delusion.)

All the koans shoot at the same experience, and in theory perhaps the answers should be interchangeable, but in the training as it has developed this experience has to be extracted from a given koan theme, and the same theme is manipulated in expressing it. A Zen teacher once explained:

In judo, sometimes a man shows the judo principle by the Nage-no-kata [a demonstration of eighteen different throws in the classical form]. The basic throwing principle is the same in all of them, but it is applied to different movements and postures; in each throw you are asked to show the appropriate application to that circumstance. No doubt an expert could find a way to apply his favourite throw to all these situations, but that is not what he is being asked to do. To keep up the judo tradition, he is asked in this demonstration to show the classical forms of the throws in the classical situations to which they apply. It is the same with a koan – one is asked to realise, and then express, the Buddha-nature through this particular theme.

There is a view that someone who is going to teach Koan Zen must have worked through a good number of different koans, so that he has himself experience of all the main groups which he may have to set to different types of pupil; but one whose Zen is for his own life alone needs only to realise it, whether through several koans, or one koan, or perhaps through no koan at all.

In eleventh-century China big collections of koans were made, and verses, discourses and short ejaculatory 'comments' were added to them. Some teachers in the Rinzai sect stressed the use of a koan, whereas in the Soto sect it was merely one means of focusing a very active mind. However there was no rigid distinction; it was more a difference of style between the two sects. Both the great masters presented in the present book were of the Rinzai sect; one of them took only one koan during his training, and the other had two. Daikaku mentions the koan as a means to meet very disturbing pressures of thought, but he clearly does not think it is essential in every case; in his Zazenron classic he does not mention it at all. Bukko makes much more of the koan practice, but he adds that if the koan is not solved within five years it should be dropped, and he does not recommend taking another one instead.

When these two teachers brought their Zen to Japan, they found that many of their pupils at Kamakura, the military capital, did not know enough Chinese to be able to master the verses and discourses that went with the classical Chinese koans; so they used two or three classical koans but also developed a system of 'on-the-instant' Zen, where something about which the pupil had a 'concern' was made into his koan. It is likely that at first a pupil had only one of these 'on-the-instant' koans, and then one of the classical ones, to complete his training. However the lines as they developed generally gave six or seven koans before a pupil finished. According to the investigations of Imai Fukuzan, 'on-the-instant Zen' lasted at Kamakura till the end of the sixteenth century. Afterwards, classical koans were given from the beginning, but by this time the whole current of Rinzai Zen was becoming weak, though a few geniuses appeared like meteors from time to time.

Early in the eighteenth century, Hakuin re-shaped the whole system, and almost all the Rinzai Zen lines today derive from him. A pupil takes something like 200 koans in his training; the first one is nearly always 'no Buddha-nature in the dog', 'the sound of one hand' or 'the original face before parents were born'. The others mostly come from eleventh-century Chinese collections like Hekiganshu, from the Rinzairoku, and especially from a collection of koans called Kattoshu. There are also about 150 ancillary koans which a teacher gives at discretion – a few of the 'on-the-instant' koans survived in this category.

There are said to be 1,700 koans, and there is a fat dictionary of them. Besides the main ones, there are supplementary tests called sassho or satsumon, which are used to clarify and strengthen a realisation which is not yet firm, or which the pupil cannot yet properly express. In the judo example given before, the shizentai is normally with the feet level and the arms hanging down. Someone who could adopt it correctly, perhaps by mere imitation, would then be asked as a sassho, 'What is shizentai with the right foot forward?' A mere imitator would be bewildered by this; but someone who had realised the usual shizentai would be able to put the right foot forward and at the same time maintain the distance between the feet and the weight distribution which are the essence of the posture.

The koans have been analysed into seventeen main themes. Some masters believe that the system has become too elaborate, and that teachers allow passes too easily, so that pupils have not really plumbed the koan to the depths. This necessitates further crises round new koans. These masters favour a complete penetration into one koan and its attendant sassho; they say that to pass the forty-eight sassho of the 'sound of one hand' koan, or the forty-two of the 'dog' koan, is to have passed through all the koan themes.

For instance, there is a famous koan called 'one finger'. A teacher used to hold up one finger in reply to all inquirers, and his boy disciple began to imitate him. One day the master cut off the boy's finger. The boy ran away. The master called him, and when he looked back, the teacher raised one finger. The boy mechanically began to do his usual imitation but found he had no finger to raise, and had a flash of realisation. In this story a form of expression is imitated blindly; then the possibility of the imitation is cut off. It is echoed in one of the sassho of the 'one hand' koan: 'when the one hand is cut off, what then?' Like a good chess problem, the koan does seem to be impossible of solution. But there is one. Thinking and thinking, the student finds his thoughts trying one avenue after another, and he presents his answers in the regular interviews with the master twice a day (or more often during a training week). The master refuses them, but not all are equally wrong. As he goes deeper, the master may hint, getting nearer'. Following this indication, the pupil presses on until his thought of the koan continues unbroken for long periods. He has no more answers; he seems to have tried them all. In monastery slang this stage is called 'wringing out'.

Suddenly he gets a tiny glimpse of something, something in his own experience which he had hitherto not noticed. It generally vanishes almost at once. He has to press hard now, and the master gets him on by encouragement, or, if he sticks and there is no other way, by force. Finally he comes upon the classical answer, or somewhere near it. When he presents it, question and answer follow like lightning, and if he wavers in his realisation the master sends him out at once. He may grasp the main line of the koan but stick for a long time at one of the sassho tests, because he cannot give it from the right spiritual state – he cannot show the proof, as it is said.

Traditionally no direct help is given with the answer, either by the teacher or a senior disciple. In fact so-called help is a hindrance. For example, the 'no Buddha-nature in the dog' koan is said to refer to the universal Dharma-body. If a disciple is told this when he enters on the koan, it distracts him. When he is beginning to move towards an answer, the thought comes up, 'And is this answer related to the Dharma-body?'

The thought hinders, because he thinks the answer has to fit in with some concept he has of the Dharma-body. And it does not. When he finally gets the true answer, he will find that his notion of the Dharma-body was wide of the mark, so that trying to conform to it held him up. Only when he thinks, '*This* is it!' and does not care whether his answer relates to the Dharma-body or not, will he have a firm hold of it.

Pupils normally see the master twice a day but during the Zen special training weeks, held at least seven times a year, four times. A Zen training week is severe. Very little sleep is allowed; some temples allow none at all during the training week at the beginning of December called Rohatsu, which ends on the anniversary of Buddha's illumination. The pupils cannot make their replies casually; in a traditional training hall there is quite a bit of beating of those who are slack in their efforts. A real master brings his students to a state where they feel their very life depends on the right answer. This is a duplication of the Buddha's resolve: 'Either I will solve the problem, or I will fall dead on this meditation seat.'

A well-known twentieth-century master was Iida Toin, who wrote a much-studied commentary on the Mumonkan koan collection. In 1934 a book of his essays was published, and one of them is concerned with sassho. His view that it is better to take one koan with all its sassho than to take many koans is similar to the early Zen which is presented in this book, and I here translate his essay on the sassho of the 'one hand' koan.

The koan of the One Hand was Hakuin's spiritual sword, and many were those who were driven by it to give up the body and lose their life. Students today suppose it is easy to solve compared with the koans of the Hekiganshu and other collections, but that is a great mistake. Those Hekigan koans and the others are all nothing but transformations of the One Hand. If you have the One Hand really in your grasp, the others are child's play – all 1,700 of them solved in a flash. People make their mistake because they haven't really grasped the One Hand. Take for instance priest Gasan, who overcame thirty Zen masters and more, one after another, until he came to believe that he was invincible. Then he came to Hakuin, and under the fire of the One Hand he was stripped of all his former conviction.

It is best not to take it lightly. In our school the One Hand has forty-eight frontier gates, hard to pass. Not that there are that number of satori-realisations; it is just that imitations are so frequent that these tests are needed. These things are instruments to distinguish true from false. When one has passed those forty-eight, the 'eight hard koans' are child's play, the Five Ranks and the Ten Prohibitions, the final koans set by the teacher, all can be passed through at one stroke.

Passed, that is, by those who have really done it properly. But nowadays the Zen world is cumbered with people who don't really understand, who after getting some distance have put a pot over their heads so they can't see anything. They just know the outward form of the answers, and it's all parrot Zen and no more.

The first time the student comes out with the classical answer to the One Hand, he has not got through to the truth. He doesn't yet really believe in it himself, but simply goes to the interview and there in front of the teacher he tries it out.

His whole idea is to get the teacher to approve something, and he goes on coming to interviews in this spirit again and again. 'That one was no good, so let me try this way ... and so he twists and turns. This constant going for interviews can be good or bad. If the time of meditation is too much taken up with it, he can easily dissipate his spiritual energies. But when he feels, '*This* is it!' then he should go at once for an interview. Apart from that, it is better not to keep going in meaninglessly, taking up the time from others.

A priest of the Pure Land sect made a poem:

> The hue of the purple robe by the ear,
> And the sound of one hand by the eye
> To be perceived.

And Hakuin allowed that this was the poem of a real follower of the Pure Land sect. Again the stanza of Zen master Tozan runs:

> Wonder, wonder!
> How marvellous is the teaching of no words.
> It cannot be grasped by hearing with the ear,
> For that voice is to be heard with the eye.

Tozan had his own great satori through the sermon of no words. It is the sound of One Hand, nothing else. Well, do you hear it at this very moment? Do you hear it with the eye, do you hear it with the ear? When you are told to listen with the eye, there's a reason for it. But that great joy must be found for oneself; others cannot take it and give it to you.

Well, when you have seen the One Hand, now show the proof! Some take three years to do it, because they had not grasped the One Hand right to the end. And even when they do bring the proof, often enough it is not the real thing; but after another year at it they get right through the One Hand. ... No, not all, it's not so easy as that! The ancients spent ten years, twenty years breaking their bones against it, like Chokei who wore out seven meditation cushions in twenty years on it, and then when rolling up a blind suddenly had the great satori. Kyogen and Reiun took twenty years. Still there is no need to despair. Shakkyo did it in barely an hour under Baso, and in Japan one man did it in three days. All it needs is tremendous courage.

But if you don't strike right through to the truth, your realisation won't stand up to anything. Everywhere there are fellows who say they have seen the One Hand; they spring up all over the place like mushrooms. But there is no need to envy them; rather they are unfortunate to have been passed through prematurely by their teachers.

There was a man who came to our temple after passing through thirty-nine koans without much trouble. But we tore them all away from him and made him begin again. He said then, 'When once one's answer has been allowed as correct, one knows what it's supposed to be, and then it's really hard to throw oneself fully into the inquiry again!' The one who hasn't been let through a koan is full of unbounded hope. He's the fortunate one. But because the Bodhi-heart is not there yet, he may not grasp the notion of season and ripening. He may tire of it quickly, and run away. And because teachers are not supposed to let the pupils run away, they sometimes allow something to pass as a satori too easily, on the ground that otherwise the pupil will be discouraged. This is why Zen decays.

The ancients went to the depths of the mountains to grasp it or even half of it. People today could not even dream of those spiritual feats. 'Even half of It' — the words have deep meaning. Today there are scores claiming to be heirs to the Dharma, isn't it pathetic? Well, let it be — now the thing is: what's the proof of the One Hand? Don't think you can just come out with the classical answer again. Of the koan of the Tree in the Fore-court, Kanzan said, 'There is a chance for the robber.' If you haven't grasped the meaning of what he said, you can't display the proof of the One Hand. If you don't know it, ask of Kanzan in the depths of the Ibuka mountains. How is it, how is it?

Then there is the One Hand Cut Off. This is one of the sassho tests like the sassho of the Mu ('not') koan – 'when the Mu is burnt it turns to ashes, when buried it turns to earth.' The Hand Cut Off runs through all those, but there are few who understand it. The path out of oneself is yet far away, far. The Royal Diamond Sword of Rinzai, the Sword koan of Joshu, the time when Obaku met the shout of Baso which left his ears deaf for three days, and without thinking he stuck his tongue right out – if you haven't these in your grasp, your Hand Cut Off is no good. Then come to the teacher and be pricked into a blaze by the thorns; face it a thousand, ten thousand times. It's the envenomed drum which is death to handle, it's the feather of the fabled poison-bird. Don't take it lightly; it is terror, terror. Cutting off, cutting off! A hint of hesitation about it and you are cut in two. Daito says, 'Space is broken up into two, into three, into four'.

Then, a most difficult passage, 'Gobble the One Hand up like a little dumpling!' Perhaps that's all right is it? But then ... 'That dumpling you've gobbled up, now spit it out again!' Of all the tests that plague the students, this is the worst. Spit it out, spit it out now! It means swallowing the whole heaven and earth, and spitting them out again, and it has to be taken right to that extent. Oh, there are many who have been passed through it, but because it was not taken up to the universal Dharma-principle they never knew the sweetness of it. The great bliss does not arise; they do not attain the great peace. Unless the One Hand is penetrated to its very roots it won't do. To pass this sassho test, you must have in your hands the Eight Difficult Koans, and particularly the one about the cow which passed through the window but then the tail stuck. Or you will never understand. And if you do understand, those eight koans will be as clear to you as a little amalaka fruit on the palm of your hand, as the Indian classics say. Or again if you can understand the Hekigan koan, 'All things go back to one; what does the one go back to?' you have this also.

All koans have related ones. In a broad sense, they are all themselves merely variations, which have been split into sub-variations. This sassho test of spitting out the dumpling has many too. But if you haven't the eye, you can't recognise them. The ability to adapt to the different koans is lacking. How do you demonstrate it? 'The thousand fruits are all from the single vine of the heart.'

There are many more tests of the One Hand, but it's wrong to stuff up with koans too much – shall we leave it here? Well after all, it's said that if you eat poison then you may as well eat the dish as well, so one more.

'What is the form of the One Hand?' To clasp the hands across the breast in the formal Zen way is no answer. You won't get it unless you have really comprehended the Second Patriarch's 'I seek the mind but cannot get hold of it.' It's a bird singing that can't be heard; it's a light shining that can't be seen by the eye. Says Monju, 'The water is water and the mountain is mountain.'

When you have it, there's a further one, 'What is the satori expression of the One Hand Transcendent?' It's an agony in the heart and belly for the monks. No good just showing your palm, or saying something at random to imitate free illumination, or to say 'Transcendent!' When the solution comes to you, you'll say, 'Why of course!' But the inspiration of heaven mustn't be divulged – the cloud ranging sage lost his power to fly through doing that. For ages I wandered blindly under an error, but today I have come to see the ice within the fire. Said Daito, 'Over thirty years I lived in the fox-hole; now I have changed to the human estate.' If you have a grip of the koan 'Not yearning after the sages, not making much of self spirit', then you get the expression of Transcendence at once. But though you have done the most advanced koans, of the Five Ranks or the Ten Prohibitions, perhaps you will still not pass this Transcendence koan.

By travelling, at last you come to the source of the river;
By sitting still, in the end you see a cloud forming.

This essay by Master Iida has been given at length because it gives a good idea of the traditional presentation of koans and sassho. One problem with the system is to make the koan living. The stories may be about what happened in China centuries before, requiring long explanations about the personalities concerned and about the trappings of the story – hossu fly-whisk, dragon and so on. As a result there may be a loss of impact. The associations of dragon in the West are quite different from those of the Chinese dragon (as it is translated), and so with the snake and many others. The problem of the story becomes remote. Many of the classical koans are like children's stories. A man put a little gosling in a jar and brought it up there, so that in the end it was too big to get out through the mouth of the jar. How did he get it out without killing it or breaking the jar? A Zen master comments on this that it is obviously absurd. How could a man ever bring up a gosling like that? It would die. Anyway, why would he want to try to do it? A fairy story – ridiculous, ridiculous. The modern man sees that, and dismisses the whole thing. What he doesn't see is how equally absurd it is that universal consciousness should be shut up in a bag of flesh and bones. And yet that is what he experiences in his own life. In spite of all he may say, when it comes to the point, that is his experience. He is *living* in the fairy story – ridiculous, ridiculous.

When a man is comfortably situated in life, it may take a good deal of talking and reading to bring one of these old koans into action. It can be done more easily if he enters a teacher-pupil relationship in an established tradition, where the strength of the teacher and tradition can jolt him out of his easy assumptions. An external crisis may achieve the same result, which is why some Zen teachers believe that crisis situations are favourable for Zen, especially crises of fear or grief.

When Zen came from China to Japan in the thirteenth century, one of the greatest centres where it flourished was Kamakura, the military capital. The lay pupils were often warriors, who had little or no Chinese and could not study Chinese Zen classics. Moreover the teachers were Chinese who knew little Japanese. So it was very difficult to establish a background of historical and Buddhist associations in which the classical koans could catch alight. The Chinese teachers began to set as koans some situation right in front of their pupils – something which disturbed them, or on which they were concentrated. In the case of the eighteen-year old military ruler Tokimune, it was fear of the coming Mongol invasions. In the case of others, it was the difficulty of reading the sutras in Chinese, for there were no Japanese translations as yet. For them the koan became, 'Reduce the sutra to one word. What is that word?'

With some of the women pupils, it was tasks like polishing, a mirror (as at Tokeiji temple) or anything else. Polished wood plays a great part in Japanese interiors, and that wood was polished by hand without wax or other aid. Over the years the surface of the wood changes; there is an old staircase in Kyoto which is like a mirror. What is now called ikebana or flower arrangement had its origin in arranging flowers in the hall for a Buddhist ceremony; flower arrangement was set as a koan from early days of Zen in Kamakura.

All these early pupils, men and women alike, lived under the shadow of the great storm-cloud of Mongol power which was building up on the mainland during the whole thirteenth century. Near the end of the century two great invasions burst on Japan, and the Japanese were preparing themselves for a third which Kublai wished to mount but finally abandoned. It was a long time before Japan could count itself free from this threat. The Zen was a Zen of crisis, at first external and then internal as Japan broke into civil war when the Mongol threat was over. As long as fighting lasted, Kamakura Zen continued; when the country was finally unified and the long era of peace began under the Tokugawas, Zen of crisis almost died out.

But some of the koans of Kamakura 'on-the-instant' (shikin) Zen gradually changed into the 'Ways'. This Zen has the advantage that the koan problem of polishing a mirror, for instance, comes up in the life of each woman pupil as a living reality; it is not a story that has to be vivified by the teacher. The koan of bringing the brush on to the paper for the first stroke of writing or painting, of meeting a fencing opponent who is known to specialise in a particular attack, of facing the cold on a winter morning – all these things were living experiences which could easily be charged with Zen inquiry.

Most people strap-hanging in a bumpy bus or train are thinking either of the place where they have come from, or the place where they are going to, either of the past or of the future. But a keen Zen man is concentrating his attention on the tanden centre just below the navel, and tries to keep his balance without relying on the strap more than necessary. He reckons his progress over a month by how many times he has to use the strap to preserve balance. He makes the occasion a part of his training, though to an outsider he is no different from anyone else. In the same way, on-the-instant Zen seeks to take the ordinary events of life as a field of training, or in the Zen phrase the place of the way' (dojo). The tanden practice is a great help in the training in fencing, calligraphy, polishing or any other physical activity, because it speeds up the process of coming to feel the body as a unity. It is practised by Zen pupils for other reasons as well, notably to develop energy and courage for the training and inquiry, which cannot succeed without them.

To give an idea of how these koan themes are handled, here is an incident reported by Master Teizan of an encounter between Takamori Saigo, then one of the most important men in Japan, and Dokuon, the famous teacher at Shokokuji, Kyoto. This was in 1869, when many Kyushu warriors were in Kyoto seeking for 'sudden-realisation Zen'. Saigo was very fond of dogs, and he appeared at the porch of the temple accompanied by an enormous dog. At the sudden appearance of this great man, the gate-keeper was overcome and hastened to call Master Dokuon, who came out to the porch to meet the visitor.

Saigo stared at the dog with his great eyes glittering and said,

'Is there Buddha-nature in the dog or not?' The teacher called out loudly, 'General!'

Saigo turned and looked at him.

The teacher said, 'There or not?'

Saigo bowed in silence and went straight back without entering the temple.

The teacher watched him go and remarked, 'A good soldier goes straight to it. If he meditates on this sassho meeting, he will have a realisation.

Finally, here are a few remarks recorded by a modern master, Tsuji Somei, in his (unpublished) autobiography, which he has kindly given me permission to quote. They were comments by his own teacher at Enkakuji:

'If you are allowed to pass the barrier of the first koan prematurely, your progress through the succeeding barriers will be anything but easy; you will often get bogged down. It is like putting your hand into a cask of liquid lacquer – it remains sticky for a long time.'

'However many interviews you may have, and however many koans you may resolve, it is nothing unless you attain perfect peace of mind.'

'However many solutions of koans you may have to your credit, it is of no avail unless you can enter into the "no-thought meditation". In that meditation there is neither mind nor body, no objects of the five senses, still less any Zen koan.'

'There has to be the freedom to enter, and to come out from, the world of the absolute or of the relative, at will.'

Mushin

Mushin (without heart, without mind) means: (1) complete cutting off of the thought-streams; (2) freedom from unnecessary thoughts while engaged in some activity. There are those who disregard the first as some sort of exaggeration, but it is clear that Daikaku and Bukko meant it literally. Westerners who identify consciousness with thought, which is only a movement in it, tend to think that absence of thought would be something like deep sleep or a total annihilation – there would be nothing left at all.

Zen teachers are not much concerned with this objection on the intellectual plane; they are concerned with it on the emotional plane, when it seems to a student on the brink that mushin would be a great death. All the koans are designed to wrap thought and feeling into one bundle, which is then thrown out.

Something remains, provisionally described in terms of immensity of space, bright like the blue sky. Students who are convinced of the importance of intellectual approval in these things, will not easily find grounds for it in Zen. From the Zen point of view, intellectual assent to the possibility of mushin experience, before the experience is actually had, is never firm; the basis of practice has to be faith in the teacher and in the tradition.

Still, intellectual people are bothered by the fact that the true nature is said to be always known, to be knowledge itself, and yet to be unknown. There is an example from another tradition (an intellectual one) which shows how something may be experienced but not consciously identified till everything else is removed. Ask someone to describe a landscape he is looking at, and he specifies the things in it. He is told, 'Something left out!' He describes smaller details. Still it is 'Something lacking!' He goes into the minutest details, but finally gives up. Now he is asked to close the eyes to a mere slit, and describe what he sees. He says, 'Only light.'

He is told, 'Didn't you see light when you were looking at the landscape? By that light you saw everything, and in fact all you saw was light. But you never included light among the things you described. Now look again.'

'Oh, *that*!' he says. 'Yes, it is so.'

This is only an analogy and cannot be pressed too far. But it serves for one point, which is that what is provisionally called consciousness, or the true nature, is independent of thought. When thinking disappears there is not nothing, but awareness of something which was in a way known all along; there is recognition in the form, 'Oh, *that*!' (not of course a verbalised thought). The first experience of it may not last very long, but it changes the basis on which life is lived; some teachers call it a glimpse beyond life and death.

Mushin means literally without thought. It has the second sense of being free from unnecessary thoughts when engaged in things of the world, so that there are actions but no inner reactions. Some Japanese teachers compare this form of mushin to a sneeze; you do not make up your mind to sneeze, you just sneeze. Though theoretically you could check it, you do not do so but just sneeze. You do not think, I am sneezing; you just sneeze. Western people hearing this often want to say, 'Do you just build a house without thinking? Don't you consider where to put it, what materials to buy, whether the rainy season is about to begin?'

Mushin in the second sense does not mean no thoughts, it means no inner reverberation of thought. The location of the house and material and season are considered, but there is no anxiety, no ambition, and once the due consideration is over, they are forgotten. An early Chinese incident exemplifies this aspect of mushin. One of the ancient worthies, a great scholar, had a distant cousin's boy staying with him, who contracted a fever. The scholar knew the treatment and applied it. He got up three times during the night to see that the treatment was taking its proper course, but between these visits he slept soundly. On another occasion his own son was staying with a relative a good distance away. A traveller who had just come from there told him that when he left, the son had a fever. The scholar was unable to sleep all night, though he could do nothing.

In the first case he was active but there was no 'extra' thinking; in the second case, though he could do nothing, there was. The first was mushin, and the second was not.

To aim at mushin is a paradox, because the aim itself would be ushin or 'with-thought'. As the questioner says in the 'Zazenron', surely it would be like trying to wash off blood with blood, to get rid of thought by thought. Daikaku says that it is in a way like thinking, but this is a right thought which cuts thought. Mushin is not annihilation of awareness, though it cuts off thought; it is compared to a vast clear sky with no cloud in it. From the point of view of Zen, deep sleep and similar states are not mushin; the darkness is just as much 'thought' as any other thought.

As with some other knotty points in Zen training, this one can be partly cleared up by a physical parallel. There are people who are continuously moving their bodies, in habitual tension; in a sense they feel that unless they are moving, they do not exist. Some are identified with speech; they keep up an incessant flow of talk, whether anyone is listening or not and irrespective of whether they have anything to say or not. Others constantly busy themselves over trivial self-imposed tasks; keeping occupied against what Kipling called 'the edge of nothing'. Even in necessary activities, these people make many unnecessary movements. They have no love for what they are doing; their love is for movement itself.

It is quite difficult in such cases to give them an idea of what relaxation means. Even in sleep such people are not relaxed. They try to lie still in imitation of relaxation, but their bodies and nerves are tense. They may keep silent, but their brains are boiling with unuttered words. They perform loosening-up exercises, but in stiff jerks. Some of them seek temporary relaxation through alcohol or other poisons, but it is no use to them because the tension returns the next day, and the body condition has worsened.

A teacher has various means of overcoming habitual tension and agitation. Relevant to Zen training are: making them temporarily impossible, and wearing them away. They are made temporarily impossible by tiring the pupil out; while he can still make a comment on how tired he is, he is not yet really tired, but when he becomes silent, when he can no longer make his favourite body twitches, the teacher lets him rest. Then for a time there is relaxation. Afterwards the teacher tells him to think and feel back to that experience, and use it as a standard when doing his relaxation exercises.

This is done in the Zen training weeks which are mostly meditation sitting with little or even no sleep, depending on the temple. After the third or fourth day the inner agitations quieten down, and the sleepy feeling also dies down. On the eighth day the participants do not drop exhausted into sleep; some of the young monks wrestle in the Sumo pushing style.

The other method is to get a tense man to lie still for long periods. For a good time he is internally full of impulses to keep shifting, but if these are not expressed they gradually die away.

In both these methods the pupil becomes aware for the first time how much effort it costs to continue the body movements. Once he has a sense of that effort, he can easily drop it. Before he realises it, the effort is to keep still: afterwards he realises that it was the movements that were an effort, and he can drop them without effort.

In the same way thinking meaningless thoughts is at first felt as natural, indeed as existence and consciousness themselves. To drop the casual thoughts requires an effort, or rather, it seems to require an effort. Afterwards the casual thoughts are realised to have been merely mental twitches, and Zen students feel the relief of mushin.

Like relaxation, mushin has the two meanings. If we say 'Do it in relaxation' we do not mean without any effort at all, but we mean without unnecessary effort. Relaxation also means complete abandonment of effort, in a lying position. In the same way, to do a thing in mushin means doing it without casual thoughts about profit or loss, or what sort of figure one is cutting, and so on. But mushin also means, and more properly, a state alert and aware of itself but without a thought. Coming out of this state, he becomes aware of the cosmic life and his actions are in harmony with it.

The wave

Hokusai's famous picture of the wave shows men and boats and Mount Fuji. The men and their efforts are details in the great surge of nature.

There are four special points from the Zen standpoint:

(1) Children think the wave is a *thing*, a separate body of water moving over the surface of the sea, and different from the other waves and from the sea itself. When they are taught to observe carefully, they find there is nothing to be distinguished as a separate wave; the wave is a moving phenomenon in the great sea. It still makes sense to speak of a wave, but only as a theoretically separate entity.

(2) The wave is about to crash on the boats and on Mount Fuji.

(3) The wave cannot crash on Fuji because Fuji is far distant, though it looks as if it is under the wave.

(4) There is no paper in the boats, in the sea, on the mountain or in the sky. Search for it and it cannot be found. But they are all nothing but paper. In fact there is no movement, no distance, no wet or dry, no life or death.

Points (2) and (3) frequently come up in the 'chakugo' or Zen comments on the koan riddles.

Hokusai's 'The Wave.'
(International Society for Educational Information, Tokyo)

Dragon-head snake-tail

In Chinese mythology the dragon is the transcendent, which lives in watery depths but mounts the heavens at times of storm, showing itself as the flash of lightning tearing the blackness of the clouds. To the snake's eye (what we should call the worm's eye) the dragon head is strange and awe-inspiring; it is supported by a mighty body and huge claws which rend the thick clouds of relative experience.

There is a phrase, 'dragon-head snake-tail' – a thing of magnificent promise which tails off abruptly. Some great phrase like 'heaven and I of one root', or 'clear and bright for ten thousand miles', is a dragon head. But if the life, including the way of uttering it, are not in accord with the phrase, it has a snake tail. A dragon's body must back up the dragon-head phrase, showing strength and inspiration, not necessarily in dramatic posturings but in contributing to life in spite of colossal disadvantages of character or circumstances, with inner freedom and calm light which sees the defects but is not overwhelmed by them. If there is this inner light and freedom, it is a real dragon; the words have their support not from other words, but from life itself. In fact, words themselves are then unnecessary.

Shunpo Roshi of Daitokuji temple collected many of the old temple records from all over Japan and found seventy-two accounts of public exchanges between Zen teachers and warrior pupils. This is one from Kuroda in Kyushu, where in the seventeenth century the clan lord Nagahisa, whose Buddhist name was Koshindo, had propagated Zen enthusiastically among his retainers.

In 1624 one of the annual ceremonies was held at Sōfukuji temple, at which the Zen teacher Kosu spoke on direct intuition as tested in Zen. He mentioned the interview of a famous Chinese layman with the teacher Baso in the eighth century.

An ivory tusk with the twelve Chinese astrological signs.
The tiger represents the peak of worldly power roaring its challenge
to the dragon which is the transcendent.

After the sermon there was an opportunity for the warriors to speak, and on these occasions there were many among the Kuroda retainers who used to present their views.

1. *Hidetoki*: That layman of old and our Koshindo are not different from one another.
   Teacher: How are they not different?
   Hidetoki: From the very beginning one rod of pure metal.
   Teacher: You don't have to put legs on it.

2. Chijun, who practised severe austerities, said: Shuffling along!
   Teacher: How does this heart go?
   Chijun: Pulling the cart as hard as it can, but it doesn't get there.
   Teacher: What is this pulling the cart and not getting there?
   Chijun: The great earth supports, but does not get up itself.
   Teacher: Dust about somewhere!

3. A senior named Toshiaki said: It is before the eyes.
   Teacher: How is it before the eyes?
   Toshiaki: The river shining with the moon, the pine blowing with the wind.
   Teacher: How is this river shining with the moon?
   Toshiaki: Bright and clear.
   Teacher: How is this pine blowing with the wind?
   Toshiaki: Clear and splendid.
   Teacher: After all, what is it like?

Toshiaki: Bright and clear, clear and splendid.
The teacher shouted: With these people it's still all dragon head and snake tail!

A phrase in use in Zen from early times was Maku-mo-zo! meaning 'don't have delusive thoughts!' It is found in Bansho's commentary on the Soto collection of koans called Shoyoroku, and it is said that a ninth-century Chinese master used to meet every questioner with Maku-mo-zo, Maku-mo-zo!

Daikaku wrote the phrase in three great Chinese characters, and presented it to Tokimune. It is a fine dragon head. But there needs to be a dragon body behind it.

In Japan there was a teacher who used it on every occasion in imitation of that old Chinese master. One day he roared Maku-mo-zo! at a questioner, who had a flash of understanding and made a deep bow. As he went out, one of the temple boys whispered to another,

'They say he's so clever, but I think our teacher's a bit of a fool. Always says the same thing, Maku-mo-zo, Maku-mo-zo, and that's all he's got.'

'What's that?' cried the teacher, spinning round.

'Oh,' said the boy in confusion, 'I was just saying Maku-mo-zo!'

Part Two
Kamakura Zen

The Zen tradition is said to be 'outside the scriptures, not setting up words, a finger direct to the human heart, seeing the nature to be Buddha'. It was brought from India by Bodhidharma, who came to China by sea in AD 520 according to tradition; one of the koan riddles is the meaning of this journey from the West by the patriarch (p. 158).

In China the tradition assumed certain forms which experience showed to be suited to the mind of the people. These forms were called collectively 'patriarchal Zen' as distinguished from the 'Buddha Zen' of India. Patriarchal Zen mostly concerns stories of Tang dynasty Chinese masters, which were used as koan riddles.

After several introductions to Japan, this Zen took firm root in the thirteenth century. But there was a difference between the lines founded by Japanese monks like Eisai and Dogen, who had gone to China and finally been awarded a mandate to teach, and the Zen taught at Kamakura, the military capital of Japan, by Chinese monks who mostly knew but little Japanese. Their pupils, mainly samurai and women, knew little Chinese; some of them could hardly read the sutras or the Zen stories, written in the Chinese of some centuries earlier.

Thus Kamakura Zen interviews had to be conducted with very few words, and the masters began to use not classical Chinese Zen stories but incidents in Japan itself. The Kyochuzakki (Jottings from a mountain ravine) written by Gio, a disciple of Master Daikaku, describes how the master initiated this 'on-the-instant' Zen, relating to something which happened to the pupil himself, and not something that happened long ago in China to someone else.

According to the Kamakura Zen teachers, when a country faces war, the warrior – if he is attracted towards Zen at all – has certain advantages. One of them is, that he knows his life may be lost the next day. This frees him from many bonds of worldly ambition and planning for the future, and gives his koan an urgency which a comfortable civilian may find it difficult to rouse. Hakuin, much later, repeats the point with emphasis. He remarks that a warrior can accomplish in Zen in a few days what will take a monk a hundred days to do. Some Zen priests do not care for these remarks of Hakuin, but they are repeated elsewhere also; for instance the Zen priest Tanzen was saying at nearly the same time that Zen priests had almost given up Zen, so that it remained only among the warriors. This is an interesting contrast with the traditional attitude in China, where warriors were by no means considered as specially good material for spiritual practice, and a parallel with that of India, where they were. One of the tests for passing a koan was, that it should give freedom, at least for a time, from anxiety about personal concerns, even life and death.

Kamakura Zen was sometimes called 'one-word' Zen. This was specially appropriate for warriors facing a foreign invasion, but in later centuries of peace, when there was leisure for intellectual speculation and aesthetic refinements, the single-word Zen did not hold the attention of people comfortable and secure. So Koan Zen was reshaped into an elaborate system of progressive koans by Hakuin (1685–1768), and Kamakura Zen fell largely into oblivion.

A few of the koans continued to be used in certain lines, but it was generally thought that these were all that had existed. However, it is now clear that there were at least a hundred purely Japanese koans, though not much material remains about them. The earliest collection seems to have been the Record of Kamakura Koans (Shonankattoroku); it was published in a small edition of 500 by the great Uesugi family in 1545. This contains a hundred koans, mostly referring to the earliest days of Zen in Kamakura. Nothing can be traced of this original edition today. At the end of the nineteenth century Imai Fukuzan found a few copies at Kenchoji temple, but already damaged by damp and worms. A few hand-written copies did circulate; at the end of the century one was possessed by Abbot Shunpo of Daitokuji, and another by Yamaoka Tesshu, a famous fencing master and also a fully qualified Zen teacher.

In 1926 Imai Fukuzan, a pupil of Shunpo, published a little edition from Sōfukuji. This is now very rare; I had the fortune to see and photograph what may be the only surviving copy. It is not mentioned in a survey of the literature of Zen published in 1959 under the joint supervision of Dr D. Suzuki, Dr H. Ui, and Dr Inouye Tetsujiro. Inouye, however, may have discovered the Imai booklet shortly afterwards; in 1942 he published a twelve-volume anthology of certain old manuscripts related to the warrior tradition of Japan, and included Imai's annotated text of the Shonankattoroku, which was thus preserved, though apparently unnoticed, in volume seven. Inouye thought it important, and added a special note to it.

Most of the Shonankattoroku stories are supplemented by sassho or supplementary questions, which are given when a pupil has already arrived at some sort of answer to the main koan. Sometimes what is listed as the first sassho is in fact the formulation of the koan itself. The sassho were developed by many Kamakura teachers up to the publication of the book by the Uesugis in 1543. The sassho were selected (by Master Muin) out of those in use at the time; there were of course many others.

There is a characteristic of Kamakura Zen which gives it a particular relevance for the West today. Besides their warrior pupils, the masters made some fully realised disciples among women, mainly but not entirely from the warrior class. The cases are parallel in that the warriors were too busy to study Chinese, and it was not then the fashion for any woman to study it, however accomplished she might be in Japanese literature. This meant that the Kamakura pupils, men and women alike, were unable to quote from Chinese Zen classics, but had to make their own answers. Blind quotation is the bane of Zen, and it was an advantage that the pupils could not quote. There was not even the temptation to quote; there was nothing in Japanese literature as yet, and they did not know Chinese. They had to be creative. For instance, a number of poems have been preserved which the nuns of Tokeiji presented at Zen interviews with their teachers. Some of these poems became koans in their own right. By the fifteenth century however this creativity was waning, because more pupils had some knowledge of Chinese. At one big training session at the time, it is recorded that less than half the nuns presented their own Japanese poems; the others were quoting from the anthology of Chinese Zen phrases called Zenrinkushu, just as is done today.

ZEN AND THE WAYS

Many of the warriors whose interviews are recorded in the Shonankattoroku were what was called 'nyudo', which meant that they had taken Buddhist vows and shaved their heads, though without leaving their families as a priest had to do. According to the researches of Imai among the Kamakura records before these perished in the earthquake of 1924, there were 365 names of warriors listed as having taken these vows, but Zen interviews are recorded of only 172.

Political background

The Hojo family provided the Regents, the *de facto* rulers of Japan, for well over a century after Hojo Tokimasa in 1203. It attained power by what would now be called a pre-emptive strike, but ruled in the main effectively and justly. Under the Hojos the country met and repelled two great invasions from the mainland.

The greatest figures among the Hojos, Tokiyori and Tokimune, led strict Buddhist lives, with shaven head and practising extreme simplicity. Tokiyori used to investigate the state of the country by travelling around incognito, and was widely respected and revered. When about to die, he sat in the meditation posture, wrote his 'death poem' according to Zen tradition and passed away in tranquillity.

Tokiyori and Tokimune both mastered Zen, mainly under the instructions of Chinese priests, of whom Daikaku and Bukko were the most prominent. These were of the Rinzai sect, but it is to be noted that Tokiyori had some teaching from Dogen, the Japanese founder of the Soto sect in Japan. Dogen would not stay in the military capital, and left before the year was out. Tokiyori saw nothing unusual in now continuing his training under Rinzai teachers, which shows that the distinction between the sects was not felt to be significant.

Tokimune's widow, whose Buddhist name was Shido, became a great figure in the Zen of the time, and the first teacher at Tokeiji temple, a training place for nuns. She was given the title 'Great Teacher' (daishi), by Bukko according to some accounts. But the Shonankattoroku gives a circumstantial narrative, according to which it was given to her by Chokei, a pupil of Bukko, against the initial opposition of the head monk; the head monk's final poem of approval contains a punning reference to the name Chokei (p. 157).

Japanese priests who learned Zen in China	Chinese priests who came to Japan, referred to in Shonanroku extracts	Mongols	Japan's military rulers: regents of the Hojo family	Japanese Zen nuns at Tokeiji
EISAI returned 1191 founded: Shofukuji (Kyushu) 1191 Kenninji (Kyoto) 1202 Jufukuji (Kamakura) 1202 died 1215			Tokimasa 1205-5	
DOGEN returned 1227 founded: Eiheiji (remote) 1244 died 1253		Control north China 1250		
SHOICHI returned 1241 founded: Tofukuji (Kyoto) 1255 died 1280	DAIKAKU arrived 1246 founded: Kenchoji (Kamakura) 1252 died 1268 GIO arrived 1246 4th teacher at Kenchoji		Tokiyori 1246–56 Tokimune 1268–84	
DAIO returned 1267	BUKKO arrived 1280 founded: Enkakuji (Kamakura) 1282	First invasion repulsed 1274 Second invasion crushed 1281	Nitta Yoshisada sacks Kamakura; Takatoki the last Hojo regent and hundreds of followers commit mass suicide at Toshoji temple 1333	Shido (widow of Tokimune) founded: Tokeiji 1285 Princess Yodo, 5th teacher c. 1350

Daikaku

Daikaku is the formal title of a Chinese monk named Tao Lung, pronounced by the Japanese Doryu, and also called by them Rankei. He was born in Szechuan in 1203. Then as now the people speak a dialect different from that of other regions of China. He became a monk at the age of thirteen, and visited various teachers (including Mujun, later the teacher of Bukko) without making a 'connection'. Finally he met a teacher with whom he practised for a long time. He was set the koan of the water-buffalo going through the window (all of it got through except the tail which stuck). Suddenly one day the age-old illusion vanished like morning mist and he saw the true landscape which had been hidden. This was some time before he was thirty-four, when he met Japanese monks who invited him to Japan, where he arrived in 1246.

Daikaku went first to Hakata in Kyushu, and in the next year to Kyoto where he was warmly welcomed by Japanese monks whom he had met in China. Shortly afterwards he was invited to Kamakura by Tokiyori the regent, who was the military ruler of Japan and an ardent Zen Buddhist. In 1255 Tokiyori built the great Kenchoji temple and training monastery, and installed Daikaku as the first teacher there. He was however accused of being a spy for the Mongols, and so persistent was the whispering campaign that Tokiyori moved him to Koshu for three years, before returning him again to Kenchoji.

Daikaku remained in Japan till his death in 1278. He had many pupils to hand on his Zen; two who appear in the Kamakura koan collection are Gio, who was a Chinese from

Szechuan like himself, and Chokei who became the fourth teacher at Enkakuji.

Daikaku had very little knowledge of spoken Japanese in his first years, and Imai reports that there were at Kenchoji many old records of his Szechuan Chinese taken down approximately (in the Japanese phonetic syllabary) by Japanese who did not understand it. There is an interview of his with Toyama Tangonokami which contains these words by Daikaku: 'Maku-maa-sun, maku-maa-sun, nyuzu kunrii fuya.' This was not standard Sung dynasty Chinese, but it was translated into Chinese characters later by Ri Sentoku, a Chinese living in Kamakura who was also from Szechuan. Then these Chinese characters were translated into Japanese by Endo Moritsugu, to mean, 'No delusive thoughts, no delusive thoughts! It is you who are from the very beginning Buddha.' In Japanese pronunciation these characters would read, 'Maku-mo-zo, maku-mo-zo, nyoze ganrai butsuya.'

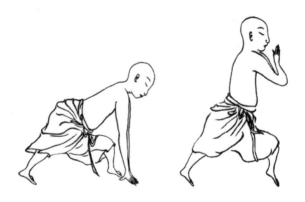

A Chinese monk exercising — reputed to be a seventh-century text.

On another occasion Daikaku was at sea in a storm, and to the anxiety expressed by other passengers he replied by laughing 'Hinten, hinten!' This was later found out to be 'Even and same' (byodo), a well-known Buddhist phrase for the state beyond distinctions.

In this and some other cases, the Chinese master repeats his phrase; there are some who believe this is still a characteristic of Chinese speech, whereas Japanese do not do it so much (except occasionally in imitation of a Chinese original). Makumo-zo (no delusive thoughts!) is a phrase often used in Zen interviews; in the Soto sect some of the teacher-pupil confrontations take place in public on formal occasions called hossen, or battle of the dharma, and this phrase is sometimes thundered out by the teacher presiding, but once only and not repeated.

The difficulty with the language was one of the causes which led to the special quality of Kamakura Zen. Very few of the Japanese pupils had a good knowledge of Chinese, and the Chinese teachers knew little Japanese. As the interviews had to take place through interpretation, they tended to be of few words. In the beginning some of the Chinese teachers set classical koans involving knowledge of the Chinese background, but later they developed a technique of creating koans out of incidents which mattered to their pupils then and there. It might seem that once the early generations of Chinese teachers had created Japanese successors, the Zen would change, but Japanese pupils tend to follow the style of their teachers very exactly, and this kind of Zen lasted over three hundred years.

For the same reason of language, the Chinese teachers did not expect the 'comment' on even a classical koan to be one of the classical Chinese poetic phrases. Their lay pupils made up their own, or quoted something they thought suitable. For instance it is recorded that Tokiyori was set the classical koan 'the tree in the courtyard', and his teacher accepted as a 'comment' a Japanese verse: 'Split open the cherry-tree and you find no colour there; yet this is the source of the spring blossoms.' After the Kamakura Zen lines largely disappeared at the end of the sixteenth century, this kind of comment was not permitted; all comments had to be from collections like the Zenrinkushu anthology of pithy Chinese phrases, which the Japanese put together for just this purpose.

Soon after arriving in Japan, Daikaku wrote a short work on Zen called 'Zazenron', which was translated into Japanese. The translation which follows is from the Japanese version. There are also some collections of his sermons, and a few extracts from these are given.

Daikaku was subject to some hostility from other sects at first, but towards the end of his life he was universally admired. A contemporary of his was Nichiren, one of the greatest figures in Japanese Buddhism though no particular friend of the Zen sect, who remarked of Daikaku: 'In Kamakura high and low revere him as a very Buddha.'

On meditation ('Zazenron')

Zazen is the gate to the great liberation; all dharmas flow out of it, and the thousand practices come from it. The divine powers of wisdom arise from within it, the way of man and of heaven opens out from it. All the Buddhas come and go through this gate, and the Bodhisattva enters his practice by it. Those of the Hinayana stop half-way, and those on the outer paths do not get on to the right road at all despite all their efforts. No doctrine, open or secret, leads to Buddhahood without this practice.

Question: What does it mean to say that zazen is the root of all dharmas?
Answer: Zen is the inner heart of the Buddha. Right conduct is his outer form, the doctrine is his word, nembutsu (mantra) is his name, but they all come from the Buddha heart and so it is their source.

Question: Zen being without form and without thought, its spiritual power does not appear, so there is no proof of its 'seeing the nature'. How can one believe all this?
Answer: It is unity of one's own heart with the Buddha heart – how can one say that spiritual power does not appear? If I do not know my own heart, how is there ever going to be proof from something else? If it is not proof enough that this very heart is Buddha, what would be proof?

Question: We are told to practise the heart way of Zen alone, but again to do many other spiritual practices and deeds of righteousness. How do these compare?

Answer: If one fully realises the Buddha's Zen, he himself is the embodiment of the six perfections and the ten thousand spiritual practices. And then, the one way of Zen is in itself all the practices. Why do you not see what is said (in the Kegon Sutra) that the three worlds are but the heart alone, and apart from the heart there is nothing else? Even if you performed ten thousand practices but did not know the heart, you could never attain realisation. And to speak of Buddhahood without realisation – how could that be?

Question: Why practise even this way? If spiritual practices do not necessarily give realisation, Buddhahood becomes uncertain. And if after all the practices the result is still uncertain, why practise?

Answer: The doctrine is profound and subtle. If once it enters the ear, in the fullness of time it will inevitably bring about wisdom awakening. An ancient has said: 'If it is heard even though not believed, that is already supreme good fortune; if it is practised though not attained, yet in the end the Buddha-fruit is had.' Zen is called the Buddha heart sect. In the Buddha heart there is from the beginning neither illusion nor realisation, and the practice of Buddhism is indeed subtle. Though realisation be not attained, a sitting of zazen is a sitting of Buddha, a day of zazen is a day of Buddha, a life of zazen is a life of Buddha. And this will be so in the future. One who merely has faith in this is a man already great in his root and in his action.

Question: If so, I ought to practise it. How is it to be done when the heart is at rest, and how when the heart is active?

Answer: The Buddha heart means no attachment for any form whatsoever. Going apart from any forms is called the true form. Of the four actions of the body, going, standing, sitting and lying down, serenity is through sitting. Sitting in meditation is the true form of thought.

Question: Please explain exactly about the true form of thought in meditation sitting.

Answer: Meditation sitting is the cross-legged Buddha posture, and the true form of thought is what is called zazen. Lock the hands in the dharma-world mudra, do not agitate body or heart, keep the eyelids covering half the pupils and the attention on the tip of the nose. See everything of cause and effect as a bubble of dream illusion, and do not engage the thought in them.

Question: Locking the legs and locking the hands is well known as the Buddha posture, but what is this half-closing the eyes and keeping the gaze on the nose-tip?

Answer: One with the eyes open sees things at a distance, the attention is distracted forcibly and the heart thrown into confusion. When the eyes are closed there is a fall into darkness, and no clarity in the heart. When the eyes are half open the thought does not rush about, body and mind are at one; in that state of clear awareness, life-and-death and the passions concerning them do not press on him. This is called becoming Buddha on the spot, the great impulse and the great action.

A student demonstrating the two meditation postures.

Question: One hears this sort of teaching, but it is difficult really to believe it. By reciting the sutras and dharanis one accumulates merit, and that gives a joy, and so with obeying the traditional ordinances like not eating in the afternoon, and reciting the name of Buddha. That all acquires merit, but just meditating quietly and doing nothing, what can there be in that?

Answer: This sort of doubt is called the result of karma, this sort of doubt is called the delusive passions. To practise all the dharmas without looking for any profit, this it is which is the profound Prajna. Prajna is wisdom, and it is a sharp sword to cut the root of life-and-death. To put down good roots in the hope of getting some good results is a delusion of a vulgar man.

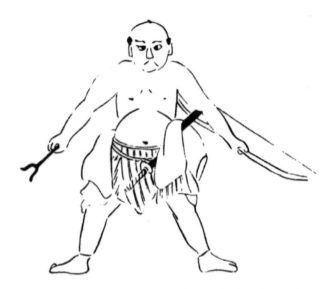

This is a symbolic picture of an archer. The gaze fixed on the nosetip
represents attention directed within – compare Zazenron (p. 68).
Not that the archer actually does turn his eyes in.

Throwing off the upper garment means no reliance
on anything external – only the original I.

The corners of the mouth turned down show attention taken down to the
tanden at the navel, and the circle around the navel represents the ki
brimming over from the navel centre to fill the whole body (p. 187).

The text says the archer is to feel 'I am the heart of the Buddha of the Sun.'

The Bodhisattva practises and puts down good roots without
seeking any results, and since his practice is from great compassion it becomes an aid to his awakening. But to practise
good in the hope of reward, little rewards on earth or in
heaven, is karma rooted in life-and-death.

Question: If the merit of good action is not accumulated, how will one ever become the Buddha, in whom all the virtues are full and complete?

Answer: If virtue and merit are accumulated, then in countless aeons he will indeed become a Buddha. But if one practises on the path of oneness of cause and effect, he is Buddha in this life. He who illumines his own heart and realises his own nature sees the Buddha which has been himself from the beginning, and it is not a question of being a Buddha now for the first time.

Question: If the one who follows 'seeing the nature to be Buddha' does not rely on cause and effect, does he then abandon doing good?

Answer: This man does do good, and the rewards of it do come to him. But that is not why he does it. The doctrine of cause and effect is taught for the upliftment of living beings, but since in fact there is no advantage for him in good actions, he does 'not take a satisfaction in them but is absolutely mushin (literally 'without-heart, without-mind') in regard to them.

Question: What is mushin? If it means absolutely without mind, then who is it who sees the nature, who is enlightened, or who teaches the doctrine?

Answer: Mushin means absolutely without that heart which is all foolishness, it does not mean without the heart which knows wrong and right. When he does not think about living beings, or long for the Buddha, or think of confusion or seek satori, or follow after the regard of the people, or hope to increase name and profit, or hate poison and injury and revenge, when he is without any thought coming up of distinctions as to good and bad, that is called a man of the way of mushin. So it is said, 'The way, without thinking, lies before the people, and the people, without thinking, tread the way.'

Question: Following sacred ordinances and prohibitions, reciting sutras and dharanis, chanting the holy name – are these of differing degrees of merit or not?

Answer: The prohibitions remove greed, and lead to a great reward in the next life. The ordinances also check the inner faults and help the growth of virtue, and the man of virtue is born in the highest place in heaven and on earth. Reciting the sutras and dharanis protects Buddhism and brings great wisdom in the next life. Chanting the name brings one to the Buddha and he will certainly be born in the Buddha land. But this mushin is the Buddha heart. The power of the Buddha heart words cannot tell, thought cannot reach; it is a great wonder.

Question: In those other things there is a particular power which is certain, but it is not clear what power there is in mushin.

Answer: Whatever powers there are in learning about the glory of the Buddha, in spreading his word, in reciting his name, all these will be in the man of mushin. If you maintain that they are not, then they are not in the other practices either. All the powers of good deeds are causes of birth in heaven or among men; mushin is the sudden enlightenment, the way of awakening. How can its power be described? It is the cause of the one great thing (Buddhahood). Passions perish of themselves, body and mind become one, this very heart is the Buddha – how could there be any doubt about it? An ancient has said, 'Rather than worship of the Buddhas of the three worlds, worship one man of the way of mushin.' This is the state where Buddha knows Buddha, and the ordinary man with his ideas of greater and less has nothing by which to judge it.

Question: None of the scriptures teaches mushin or points to it as something desirable. So why does this teaching of Zen esteem it so much?

Answer: The scriptures do teach it when they speak of cutting off words, and of what is beyond explanation, and of absolute emptiness as the cause of the one great thing. Again they teach that all things perish. Shakamuni closed his lips, Vimalakirti shut his mouth – was not this to show mushin? Bodhisattvas have already attained wisdom so the Buddha did not teach it to them, and the second path (taking many aeons) being so difficult, he did not teach that either. In the Kegon sutra it says that this sutra should not be taught to those of little wisdom, and this is the meaning. Though there are 84,000 doctrines in the holy teachings, they do not go beyond the principles of form and void. What displays any kind of shape, that is form or body. And what displays no shape, all that is the void. The body since it has a shape is called form; the heart since it has no shape is called void. No sutra goes beyond these two, form and void. The mushin state cannot be taught, or pointed to as something desirable. Words do not go there, and so it is called a 'separate tradition outside the scriptures'.

Question: Are we ourselves taken as illusion or as realisation? What is this heart, without knowing which one will not find the root and source of illusion and realisation? Is the heart inside the body or outside, and where does it come from?

Answer: The form body of the four great elements and the five skandhas fills all the directions and is the root and source of all living beings. When the causes and associations come to a focus, a physical body is produced. This is called life. When the karmic effects transform themselves again, the four great elements disappear and this is called death. The form is vulgar or holy, but in the heart there is neither illusion nor satori. Still when it temporarily goes astray it is called 'living being', and when it is realised it is called 'all the Buddha'. Illusion and realisation are just a deluded heart. In the true heart there is neither illusion nor realisation. Living being and Buddha are caused by the illusion or realisation of the one original heart. When the true nature is grasped, there is after all no distinction of vulgar and holy. So the Surangama sutra says, 'The mystical nature perfect and bright is apart from all name and form, and from the very beginning there has never been any world of living beings.'

Question: If there is no illusion in the heart nature originally, where does it come up from?

Answer: When delusive thought arises, illusion follows, and from that the passions come to be. If delusive thought ceases, illusion goes, and from that the passions also. Passions are the dharma course of life, and the seed of life-and-death; bodhi awakening is the dharma course of extinction, and the bliss of nirvana. When you are in illusion, everything is passion; when realised, everything is bodhi. The people of the world do not know this root of illusion and realisation; they suppress thoughts of life-and-death so that they do not arise, and they think this is what is intended by 'no thought arising' or mushin. But this itself is thought of life-and-death, and not mushin, not nirvana; to check thought by thought is reinforcing life-and-death.

Question: It is said that the Hinayana followers fall into a mere void and do not know mushin. Does the Mahayana bodhisattva attain mushin or not?
Answer: The bodhisattva attains ten stages, and still has the two obstacles of passion and wisdom. In the seventh stage he has still a notion of search, which itself is an obstacle. In the tenth stage he has a notion of realisation-light, and as such, this is an obstacle. But when there is right realisation, it is mushin.

Question: If a bodhisattva does not know it even in the tenth stage, how could a beginner attain this mushin?
Answer: The Mahayana is a wonder. As soon as the source of thought is cut, it is sudden satori. Buddhist philosophers have set up three grades of wisdom and ten of holiness, but this is for people of slow intelligence. One whose intelligence is clear comes to a right realisation when first his heart stirs spiritually; he attains mushin and here and now sees the nature to be Buddha. In mushin there are no distinctions at all.

Question: What does it mean, 'see the nature to be Buddha'?

What is the nature, and what is this seeing? Is it knowing through wisdom, or is it a seeing with the eye?

Answer: The wisdom attained by studying the sutras is a wisdom of distinctions, a knowledge attained through senses of hearing and seeing. In our practice, it is no use. What we call the clear-sighted eye is turning the light back and perceiving one's own original nature.

Question: So 'seeing' is knowing. But what is meant by one's own original nature?

Answer: It is the nature which all beings have from the very beginning, and which upholds them. It has always been, it is without life and without death, eternal and unchanging. This it is which is called the original self-nature. It is one and the same in all beings and all Buddhas, so it is called Buddha nature. The three treasures, living beings on the six paths of reincarnation, with this nature as their root play out their parts.

Question: What is turning back the light?

Answer: It means that the light of self which illumines all things is turned round and shone back to illumine the self within. The heartlight is like the rays of sun and moon, immeasurable and unrestricted, which illumine all regions at home and abroad. There where the rays do not reach is dark and is called the demon cave of the black mountains. All the demons live there, and they do great harm to man. The heart is just like this. The heart nature is shining wisdom immeasurable and unrestricted which illumines all regions. Where it does not reach is dark, the shadow world of ignorance. All the passions live there and they do great harm to man. The wisdom heart is bright; delusive thought is shade. When the light makes the things themselves shine, that is called illumining them. When the heart does not transform itself into states of thought but faces the original nature, that is called turning the light back, or universal shining. The field of this universal shining is a state before illusion or realisation have appeared. People today think that their delusive thoughts are their true heart, and try to be happy through the passions. How could they ever get out of life-and-death?

Question: The main point of zazen is supposed to be that no thought arises. But if we check thought by thought, surely it is like washing off blood with blood?

Answer: The original and true state of the heart is said to be no thought arising. It is not checking thought, but neither is thought unchecked. It is just that thought does not arise. If one can really come to this original state, it is called the Buddha and the dharma nature. After that there is no need even for zazen. There is no delusion and no satori – how should there be thought? And if this true state is not attained, thought will inevitably arise. Even if thought is held down forcibly, it would still all be ignorance. A stone can press the grass flat, but after a time it rises again. This point must be very deeply meditated upon – it is no easy thing.

Question: Someone has said: you must go towards the place where no thought arises. What about this?

Answer: When it is said no thought arises, it means no form of life-and-death or past or future. Life and death arise from thought and if you do not know the place where thought arises you will not know the root of life and death. Living beings all twenty-four hours are being used by the thought of passions, and going against what they really are. But if the clouds of delusive thought clear, the moon of the heart nature is revealed and the thought which before was of contemptible things changes to become pure wisdom. With this thought he teaches and instructs the living beings. Master Joshu says: 'People are used by the twenty-four hours but I can use the twenty-four hours.'

Question: You are saying that at the time of zazen it is wrong if thought arises but it is also wrong to check it, so what does one do?

Answer: Before there has been a sight of one's own nature, both thought arising and the checking of it are faults. The sutras teach no arising of delusive thought, and again no eradicating of it, and all this is to bring one to a knowledge of the original nature. When the true nature is known, practice is not needed. When the disease of illusion is removed, it is pointless to continue the treatment. However when the illness of delusive feelings does come up, use the spiritual treatment. That thought arises is the illness, that it should not be continued is the treatment.

Question: Still as thought has no self nature, even if it arises what is the fault in that?

Answer: Though it has no self nature, it is a fault if it arises. The things in a dream for instance are known to be unreal afterwards on waking, but how could one say that there is nothing wrong with a nightmare? It is setting up these faults and making dreams out of them that is the illusion of living beings. Once the Buddha law is heard and faith is roused, all is well. But people with no heart for the true way are dull in their concentration and do not realise there is anything wrong. They may suppress some of their little thoughts, but they are not aware of the great thoughts. Since they do not cut off the source of them, they may make some good karma but it is difficult for them to get free from life-and-death.

Question: You have said, do not think any thought of good or bad at all, and that having no thought of good or bad is the central point of zazen. What about the little thoughts and great thoughts of everyday life?

Answer: When it is said, do not think any thought of good or bad, it means directly cutting off. This is not to be done only at the time of meditation sitting; if you reach this state, then walking and standing and sitting and lying down are all Zen. You do not necessarily have to be in the sitting posture. The Zen master says in the Shodoka poem, that walking too is Zen and sitting too is Zen; talking or silent, moving or still, the body is at peace. A sutra says, 'Be always in it, whether in the slow Zen walking (kinhin) or sitting or lying down.' The so-called little thoughts are those that suddenly come up about things which are in front of us. The so-called big thoughts are those of greed, anger, foolishness, prejudice, pride, jealousy, fame, profit and so on. At the time of zazen, those of weak will suppress the little thoughts but the great thoughts are in their hearts without their realizing it.

Throwing away these bad thoughts is to cut off directly their root and source, and when you cut off that root and source directly, the passions become bodhi, foolishness becomes wisdom. The three poisons of greed, anger and folly become pure conduct, ignorance becomes the great knowledge of the nature. How should it not be so with the little thoughts also? This is what the Buddha meant when he said, 'If it is you that make the thing turn, that is the Buddha.' You just have to make the thing turn, and not be made to turn by the thing. You must be the pivot on which the thing turns; do not make the thing the pivot on which you are turned.

Question: If to be Buddha is to be the pivot of the thing, what is that thing, and what is the pivoting?

Answer: The thing is the ten thousand phenomena, and to be the pivot is to be released from the body, not to agitate the heart in regard to any circumstance whatever, but instead to face the true nature. When circumstances do not clog the heart, heaven and spirits and demons and gods, passions and life and death, will all be nothing to you and this is called making the thing turn. The essential point is not to let the heart be diverted by any thing. Even clinging to a Buddha or clinging to a dharma have to be cut off, how much more the delusive thoughts! Though the heart which does the cutting is in a way like a heart which is thinking, this is right thinking, the concentration which brings right vision.

Question: Passions and bodhi arise distinctly from the one heart. What is it that they come from?

Answer: Seeing forms, hearing sounds, smelling odours,

experiencing tastes, feeling touch, knowing the things – these are the powers of the five senses and mind the sixth. Distinguishing these as good and bad, judging them as right and wrong, is wisdom. To set up an individual I in this, to bring up love and aversion, is all delusive sight. By this delusive sight there is attachment to form, and this is called illusion. From this are brought up the five skandhas (form, feeling, perception, impulse, making discriminations); all this is called passion. As a result of passion there is taking bodies as living beings, and then they turn towards killing, robbing, lust, lying and so on, and finally they fall into the three lower paths, in hell or as hungry ghosts or as animals. All this comes up from delusive thought. When it arises even a little, at once turn that delusive thought to face the true nature, and then immediately it becomes mushin. If once you are able to be at rest in mushin, your body of five skandhas becomes the five-fold body of the dharma (discipline, meditation, wisdom, liberation, liberated vision). This is what the Diamond Sutra means by not letting the heart settle down anywhere as a home. If the heart is applied like this, it is the great spiritual training.

Question: If someone has the merit of having done zazen for a long time so that his concentration is matured, doubtless he will not have passions and wrong illusion in his heart. But for a beginner, how will the passions ever come to a stop?
Answer: Do not hate the passions, but simply purify your heart. An ancient has said that it takes a man of iron to train in the way. You must put your hand on your heart and then solve the riddle; do not concern yourself with rights or wrongs but go straight to the supreme bodhi-awakening.

Putting your hand on the heart means to make out what is correct and what is deluded in the heart. He who knows when his heart is astray is the wise man. When wisdom comes and illusion ceases to be, it is like bringing a light into a dark cave where the rays of sun and moon have never reached. That ancient darkness does not go somewhere else; it suddenly becomes light. When the light of wisdom comes, darkness and ignorance and passions do not wait upon their going but are gone. At night the empty sky is dark, but when the dawn sun appears that sky becomes the day, becomes bright. The heart is like that. Illusion is dark, satori bright. When the rays of wisdom shine, the darkness of passion all at once becomes bright. There is no second thing beside the bodhi.

Question: So it is by the power of wisdom that the darkness of passions is brightened, and without wisdom there is no bodhi. But how then can wisdom be obtained?

Answer: There is a light of wisdom in the self which is naturally luminous and clear, but when covered by delusive thoughts it is lost and then illusion arises. When a man sees a dream, everything in it is taken as real, but on awakening there is nothing there at all. Delusive thought is like a dream, and when regarded from the waking standpoint it has never been there. Living beings are confused and take the delusion for reality.

Question: For a long time we have no satori, and suddenly we know it; do we then know things of the past and future as well?

Answer: When delusive views have all come to an end there is a sudden awakening from the great dream, and this is perception of the Buddha nature, which is called the great satori and the great piercing through. This state is not accessible to ordinary thought based on distinctions. To know past or future is a supernatural power resulting from the power of ascetic practices and it is not to be called a great satori. Demons and devils, followers of the outer paths, mountain hermits and others may have these powers by virtue of having performed difficult and painful austerities in the distant past. They have the virtue of the practices, but if they do not give up wrong views they cannot enter upon the Buddha way.

Question: Why should one who has satori not have these powers?

Answer: This body has been built up on past illusion, and supernatural powers which relate to it are not manifested by one who has seen the nature to be Buddha. When satori comes, he shakes off the taint of the fields of perception of the five senses and the mind, and cuts off life-and-death. From that, he does have a supernatural power of inspired action. But this is not the supernatural powers of the outer path or of the demons, tainted with passion. The man of satori, which is universal, completes the Buddha way without passing through countless aeons; is that not a supernatural power? – what to say of supernatural power of inspiration which he has.

Question: 'See the nature to be Buddha' and 'the heart, the Buddha' – are these different or not?

Answer: The direct meaning of the words 'the heart, the

Buddha' is that there is no Buddha apart from the heart. Anyone who can accept this meaning directly is a man of penetrating intelligence. The other phrase 'no heart, no Buddha' also points to the same thing. 'See the nature to be Buddha' means perceiving one's own nature directly, cutting off the root of individual existence and knowing the fullness of the spiritual nature. Then there is neither life-and-death nor passion, and this is provisionally called 'to be Buddha'. It is realisation of Buddha, full realisation that there never was any illusion. There is no real difference between the two phrases, but as the way of entry is different the phrases are different in form.

Question: It is said that the nature is eternal and unchanging and one and the same in living beings and in Buddhas. Yet the living beings are in illusion with the pain of life and death. So can it be said to be one and the same?

Answer: It is one and the same under the light of wisdom, but not in the sight of ignorance. The words of the patriarchs are a tile to knock on the gate. Before the gate is opened, 'see the nature to be Buddha' is the ultimate word, but when one goes in, all forms are left behind and even to be Buddha is meaningless.

Question: All the doctrines open and secret teach these eight: teaching, principles, wisdom, cutting off, practice, states, cause, effect. The shravakas of the Hinayana have four dhyanas and eight samadhis by which they enter Nirvana of absolute extinction, not to be touched by fire, water or storm, and empty of the five skandhas. Bodhisattvas hold to the ordinances of the Mahayana, practise innumerable deeds of benevolence, pass through the three stages of wisdom and the ten of holiness, cutting off all passions within and without. If cutting off the passions is Buddhahood, how is it that the Buddhas of the three worlds leave the region of the absolute and come into the desireworld of life-and-death at all?

Answer: Buddhas and Bodhisattvas are in response to the prayers of the living beings; if there were no prayers of the living beings there would be no Buddhas and Bodhisattvas. In the Hinayana there is no such response and so the Mahayana calls it entering a liberation-abyss. The Bodhisattvas of wisdoms and holiness progress in their practices and enter the gate of freedom in everything, and to help living beings they leave the paradise of pure light and come into this world of five taints, as trees of bodhi. Just as on the uplands, clean and dry, the lotuses do not grow, but in the despised slime the lotuses do grow, so it is with them. Or take the case of agriculture. The seedlings cannot be planted in clean, dry ground, but they are put in slimy mud with dirty manure on them. So the rice is planted and in due season the sun does its work and the dews and rain bathe them and the sprouts grow, and root and stem and branches and leaves flourish in abundance. So till the rice is fully grown, the work is complete and the farmers sing the harvest song. The coming of a Buddha into the world is just like that. The Buddha law cannot be founded like a thunderbolt from a blue sky. He puts on a humble shabby vesture for his role of persuading the beings of wrong deeds and passions, he adapts his preaching to them, and plants the seed of secret virtue. In due season the sun of wisdom shines on it, the breeze of compassion fans it, the rain of dharma bathes it, the dew from heaven washes it, and the Way puts forth its sprouts, and root and stem and branches and leaves flourish in abundance. So the bodhi tree grows, and the blossoms of realisation begin to open and the fruit of final realisation appears. This is called the fulfilment of the transformations of the path, the eternal bliss of nirvana.

The man of the Way too is like the vitality of the seed of a tree. The manure of the six defilements is put in the ground and then the spiritual seed is set down in it, and the sprout of the physical body grows up, putting forth feeling and knowledge. The root of the mind develops, will and imagination expand and the branches of the conscious spirit spread wide; the leaves of spiritual desire are luxuriant. There is happiness in root and branch, the blossoms of knowledge open and the fruit of realisation ripens. After the efforts of the way, he sings the happiness of mushin.

The ordinary man also is like a seedling. In the earth of illusion the manure of desire and aversion is set, and a seed of ignorance put down; the sprouts of the skandhas grow and the passions draw sap from the deep alaya-consciousness. The root of attachment develops and the stem of egoism grows strong; twisted branches of doubt spread wide, and the leaves of jealousy are luxuriant. It becomes a tree of passion, the flowers of temptations open on all sides and the fruit of the three poisons ripen. After all the efforts for profit and fame, he sings the happiness of the five desires.

Say now, of these three kinds of tree, is one better than another or not? If there is a man who in one hand grasps the three seedlings, nourishes their root, and then all at once pulls them out and plants them in the realm of absolute sameness where there is no yin or yang, making there a bodhi tree which has no shadow, truly this will be a mighty man. Heaven and earth and myself of one root, the ten thousand things and myself are of one body. Now say, What kind of thing are you? If you can shout aloud your Buddhahood, you are far beyond heaven and earth.

Sayings of Daikaku

Zen practice is not clarifying conceptual distinctions, but throwing away one's preconceived views and notions and the sacred texts and all the rest, and piercing through the layers of coverings over the spring of self behind them. All the holy ones have turned within and sought in the self, and by this went beyond all doubt. To turn within means all the twenty-four hours and in every situation, to pierce one by one through the layers covering the self, deeper and deeper, to a place which cannot be described. It is when thinking comes to an end and making distinctions ceases, when wrong views and ideas disappear of themselves without having to be driven forth, when without being sought the true action and true impulse appear of themselves. It is when one can know what is the truth of the heart.

The man resolute in the way must from the beginning never lose sight of it, whether in a place of calm or in a place of strife, and he must not be clinging to quiet places and shunning those where there is disturbance. If he tries to take refuge from trouble by running to some quiet place, he will fall into dark regions.

If when he is trying to throw off delusions and discover truth, everything is a whirl of possibilities, he must cut off the thousand impulses and go straight forward, having no thought at all about good or bad; not hating the passions, he must simply make his heart pure.

Illusion is dark, satori is bright. When the light of wisdom shines, the darkness of passion suddenly becomes bright, and to an awakened one they are not two separate things.

This is the main point of meditation. But an ordinary beginner cannot mount to the treasure in one step. He moves from shallow to profound, progresses from slow to quick. When in the meditation sitting there is agitation of thought, then with that very agitated mind seek to find where the agitated thought came from, and who it is that is aware of it. In this way pressing scrutiny as to the location of the disturbance further and further to the ultimate point, you will find that the agitation does not have any original location, and that the one who is aware of it also is void, and this is called taking the search back.

If the press of delusive thoughts is very heavy, one of the koan phrases should be taken up, for instance seeing where it is that life comes from. Keep on inquiring into this again and again. An ancient has said, that while you do not yet know life, how should you know death? And if you have known life, you also know death, and then you will not be controlled by life-and-death, but will be able to rise or set as you will.

Hearing a sound, to take it simply as sound; seeing a form, to take it simply as form; how to turn the light back and control vision, and how to turn hearing within – these are the things which none of you understand. In hearing sounds as you do all day long, find out whether it is the sound which comes to the convolutions of the ear, or the ear that goes out to the location of the sound. If it is the sound which comes to the ear, there is no track of its coming; and if it is the ear that goes to the sound, there is no track of its going. The practiser of Zen should carefully go into this in his silent inquiry. In silent investigation, with great courage turn the hearing back till hearing comes to an end; purify awareness till awareness becomes empty. Then there will be a perception of things which is immediate without any check to it, and after that, even in a welter of sounds and forms you will not be swept away by them, even in a state of darkness and confusion you will be able to find a way. Such is called a man of the great freedom, one who has attained.

Whether you are going or staying or sitting or lying down, the whole world is your own self. You must find out whether the mountains, rivers, grass and forests exist in your own mind or exist outside it. Analyse the ten thousand things, dissect them minutely, and when you take this to the limit you will come to the limitless, when you search into it you come to the end of search where thinking goes no further and distinctions vanish. When you smash the citadel of doubt, then the Buddha is simply yourself.

The true nature is eternal and unchanging, and the same and equal in Buddhas and other beings. When wisdom illumines this sameness and equality, there is no appearance of ignorance. The words of the patriarchs are only a tile to knock on the gate; before entering, 'see the nature to be Buddha' is the ultimate word, but when inside there is no concern with any form, and 'to be Buddha' has no meaning.

A man of great faith, turning his gaze to before there are any indications to be distinguished, directing his will to where action cannot reach, taking months and years to be at ease in it, using every means to intensify it, when the time comes finds a great laugh bursting out irresistibly, and a vastness of spirit like the great sky encompassing all. Approaching people with that in his grasp, he has an infinity of means to help them. It is called the gate of great liberation, the treasure of the great light, and he finds everywhere the opportunity to demonstrate inspired action. Right it is to call this state the void, right to call it existent, and here there is no bar to praising the Buddha or laughing at the patriarchs.

The two earholes hear sounds, and how this occurs is precisely satori; the two pupils see forms, and the heart is suddenly light. Among some old priest's disciples up to eight thousand, if there is even one who when called individually does not turn his head, who when hit is not disconcerted, when that one comes to the state before sound is uttered, before forms have appeared, he will penetrate the high and low of it, and know how to return to where he stands.

When you set out to look for the way of the Buddhas and patriarchs, at once it changes to something that is to be sought in your self. When sight becomes no sight, you come to possess the jewel, but you have not yet fully penetrated into it. Suddenly one day everything is empty like space which has no inside or outside, no bottom or top, and you are aware of one principle (ri) pervading all the ten thousand things. You know then that your heart is so vast that it can never be measured. Johoshi says, 'Heaven and earth and I of one root; the thousand things and I are one body.' These words are of burning import and absolutely true.

The holy men and illumined ones who have this principle clear in them, find that past, present and future are like dream-stuff. Wealth and rank, gain and fame are all an illusion; the mined gold and heaped-up jewels, the beautiful voices and fair forms, are illusion; joy and anger and sorrow and happiness are this illusion. But in all this illusion there is something which is not illusion. When even the universes crumble, how should that crumble? When at the end of the world cycle the universal fire blazes everywhere, how should that burn? That which is not illusion is the true being of each and every man. Every day go into the calm quiet where you really belong, face the other way and turn your gaze back; if you do this over the long years, that which is not illusion will of itself reveal itself before you. After that manifestation, wherever you stand Miroku is there, and when you turn to the left or glance to the right, it is Shakamuni everywhere.

Realisation makes every place a temple; the absolute endows all beings with the true eye. When you come to grasp it, you find it was ever before your eyes. If you can see clear what is before your very eyes, it is what fills the ten directions; when you see what fills the ten directions, you find it is only what is before your eyes.

It is not, as some ancients and the Confucians taught, that you sweep away ordinary feelings and bring into existence some holy understanding. When ordinariness and holiness exist no more, how is that? An octagonal grindstone is turning in empty space; a diamond pestle grinds to dust the iron mountain.

The transcendent impulse is not from a source outside; the awareness of it is to be sought in movement and stillness both. When suddenly movement and stillness both cease to be, the vast blue ocean is dried up in one gulp.

Bukko

Bukko Zenji (Zen master Buddha-light) was a posthumous title conferred, by the Japanese Emperor, on a Chinese monk whose name was Tsu yuen, pronounced by the Japanese Sogen. He has also the names Mugaku, Shigen and some others. In this book he is called simply Bukko. He was born in 1226, and as a child was always fond of temples and Buddhism. One day when he had accompanied his father to a temple and was playing in the garden, he heard a monk chanting the verse from a famous Taoist classic called Saikondan:

> The shadow of the bamboo sweeps the steps,
>> But the dust does not stir;
> The moon's disc bores into the lake
>> But the water shows no scar.

This verse seized on his mind, and he finally made up his mind to renounce the world. When his father died next year, he became a monk, at the age of thirteen. The next year he climbed the Kinzan mountain and put himself under the Zen master Mujun. As it happened there were Japanese monks there at the same time. When he was seventeen, this teacher set him his first koan, 'no Buddha-nature in the dog'. He determined to resolve this in one year, but he could not come to an understanding of it, nor in a second year either. It was the same until the sixth year, when he was twenty-two. He could now sit in profound meditation for long periods without fatigue; finally he reached a state where in the sky and on the earth there was only this one character Mu ('no') everywhere, and even in his dreams it was the same. Then a senior monk told him to drop the Mu, but he could not separate himself from it. After a good time, he was sitting in meditation when the Mu disappeared, and his body-consciousness along with it. There was only an immensity of space, rid of mental cogitations; he says it was like a bird escaped from a cage. The body and mind were paralysed and his fellow monks thought he was dead, but a senior monk told them that this was a samadhi state in which the breath stops for a time. If the body were kept warm and covered, and looked after, it would revive of itself. After a day and night empirical consciousness returned. One night after this, he was sitting on the bed in deep meditation, when the head monk hit the board with a mallet in one of the usual temple signals. As Bukko heard it, the blow struck through to the 'original face' and it appeared to him. When he closed his eyes there was a vast expanse of space, and when he opened them he saw everything in this vastness. He could not contain his joy and jumped from the bed to run out under the moon. He looked at the sky and cried, 'How great the universal dharma-body! From the very beginning vast as it is now!' He presented a poem of realisation to the teacher Mujun:

> One hammer-blow smashed the spirit-cave,
> And out rushed the Titan unabashed!
> Ears as deaf and mouth as dumb,
> Yet one careless touch and a meteor shoots away.

Mujun did not confirm this as good but neither did he dismiss it as wrong. He simply set him another koan, the enlightenment verse of Kyogen. (Kyogen attained enlightenment after many years of Zen, when a stroke of his broom dislodged a stone which struck against a tree. The first line of the verse is: One stroke and I forgot all I knew.) The next year Mujun died; after some time Bukko found a new teacher and came under his hammer. One day he was drawing water from the well and as the pulley turned freely there was in him an uprush of realisation. The Kyogen verse and the Mu koan were as clear as the palm of his hand. He was then thirty-six. He refused some attractive offers and retired to a hermitage near his native village, where he took a few pupils and also looked after his old widowed mother in her last years. He was there seven years. After she died he went to the Zen centre on Tendo mountain, and there met an envoy from Tokimune, who invited him to Japan, where he arrived in 1280.

From the above summary it appears that Bukko attained his final realisation through only two koans. The first one he continued for six years, during which time he became an expert in samadhi trance meditation. His experience of an immensity of space like a vast empty sky is a well-known one in Zen, and is counted one of the most favourable indications. It is referred to again and again in Zen biographies. In his case it was experienced first when body and mind were lost sight of; later it appeared whenever he closed his eyes, and even when they were opened he had this awareness of limitless space containing everything. (This last experience is so common in Zen accounts of realisation that it was made the subject of a paper at the International Congress of Psychology in Tokyo, 1972; variations of the satori space experience were discussed, of course only in neuro-physiological terms as a postulated change in the body image.) It is to be noted that the teacher neither disapproved nor approved of this expressly, but set the second koan.

When the Mongols were extending their conquests over China, a group of them broke into the Noninji temple where Bukko was living. He sat down in the meditation posture as the soldiers came up to him with drawn swords, and recited a poem:

In heaven and earth, no crack to hide;
    Joy to know the man is void and the things too are void.
Splendid the great Mongolian longsword,
    Its lightning flash cuts the spring breeze.

The Mongols were impressed with his courage and left him alone.

When he was in Japan, Bukko fell ill and the doctors recommended the mogusa cautery, if he could stand it. In this treatment, little pinches of the herb are placed on the body, often in a line on either side of the spine, and are set alight. Before the operation, a busy-body inquired, 'Is this cautery to be applied to the individual body or to the universal dharma-body? If it is to the individual body, well, a Zen master knows that he is the universal body, so he will not be affected by it; and if it is to be applied to the universal body, why, the universal body is not ill.'

Bukko replied in a verse:

Fire, and the whole body ablaze!
Every mote in the air and every grain of earth aflame.
The old monk endures it for no other purpose than this:
That the spiritual illness of all living beings be healed.

Bukko was in Japan only six years, and he never learned Japanese well. What he said was taken down phonetically, if no interpreter was present, and translated later. Imai Fukuzan, who examined and analysed many of the old records at Enkakuji and Kenchoji before they were largely destroyed by the great earthquake in 1924, said that many of these notes still remained. It is clear that the scribe often did not understand them at all – one which was preserved along with the others long remained a riddle, but in the end turned out to be, 'Come in, come in! I have something to say to you.'

Bukko was the inspirer of the regent Tokimune, who was his devoted pupil; after Tokimune's forces had repelled the second Mongol invasion Bukko had the desire to return to China to die there, but put it off at the entreaty of Tokimune.

Bukko had a Chinese sense of humour, which may sometimes have been a puzzle to his pupils. In the koan about seeing a dragon (p. 123) Bukko quoted the traditional figure of twenty-one days for the meditation retreat. He must have seen his hearers, from a people not naturally patient, making their mental calculations something contrary to the spirit of Zen. So he concluded, 'If you can't see it on the twenty-first day, practise for twenty-one weeks. And if you still do not see it, then press your practice on for twenty-one years, all hours of the day and night, never forgetting your vow, and when the last day comes you will surely meet a dragon.'

Another example of humour, containing deep spiritual instruction, was a short 'sermon for the librarian'. He said that in China a monk used to sit in meditation in the library but never read any of the books. The librarian asked why he did not use them, and the monk said, 'I cannot read the characters.'

'You can ask me to read them for you,' said the librarian.

The monk stood up with his hands clasped across his breast in the formal Zen standing posture, and said, 'What character is this?' The librarian had no reply.

Outline of Bukko's teachings

The way out of life-and-death is not some special technique; the essential thing is to see through to the root of life-and-death. That root is not something that fell from heaven or sprang up from earth; it is at the centre of the functioning of every man, living with his life, dying with his death, becoming a Buddha, making a patriarch. These are all in dependence on it, and one who goes into Zen has to pierce and break through to this thing.

What is called Zen sitting is not some sort of operation to be performed, and to take it so is wrong. In our line, it is simply realizing what one's own true heart really is, and it is necessary to pledge oneself to the true heart.

Going into Zen is seeing one's original nature, and the main thing is to make out what one was before even father or mother were born. For this he must concentrate his feeling and purify it, then eliminating all that weighs on his thought and feeling, he must go to grasp the self. We are saying that the self seeks to grasp the self, but in fact it is already the self, so why should it go to grasp the self? It is because in the mass of knowings and perceivings and judgments, the true self is always so wrapped up in the distinctions and exclusivities that it does not get out to show itself as it is.

It may be asked, how is the self to be approached? By looking into it through this sort of inquiry: forty years ago where did it come from, and a hundred years hence where will it have gone to? and right now, who is the person who is making the inquiry? that true face which was before father and mother were born, where is it right now? when suddenly one day the light of life, now so brilliant, will be withdrawn, where does it go to? In this sort of way look into the self. Look when you sleep, look when you sit, look when you walk. When you find you cannot look any more, then you must look and see how that inability to look appears and disappears; as you are looking how the sight comes and the sight goes, satori-realisation will arise of itself.

At the beginning, you have to take up a koan. The koan is some deep saying of a patriarch; its effect in this world of distinctions is to make a man's gaze straight, and to give him strength as he stands on the brink of the river bank. For the past two or three years I have been giving in my interviews three koans: 'the true face before father and mother were born', 'the heart, the Buddha,' and 'no heart, no Buddha'. For one facing the turbulence of life-and-death, these koans clear away the sandy soil of worldly concerns and open up the golden treasure which was there from the beginning, the ageless root of all things.

However, if after grappling with a koan for three or five years there is still no satori, then the koan should be dropped, otherwise it may become an invisible chain round him. Even these traditional methods can become a medicine which poisons. In general, meditation has to be done with urgency, but if after three or five years the urgency is still maintained forcibly, the tension becomes a wrong one and it is a serious condition. Many lose heart and give up as a result. An ancient has said, 'Sometimes quickly and sometimes slowly, sometimes hot on the trail and sometimes resting at a distance.' So this mountain priest now makes people at this stage throw down their koan. When it is dropped and there is a cooling down, in due time they hit on what their own true nature is, as the solution of the koan.

This mountain priest himself formerly went through all these states, and as it is said, the man who has had a serious illness knows well the treatment which saved him; it is what one knows by experience that can be communicated to others. In concentration on a koan, there is a time of rousing the spirit of inquiry, there is a time of breaking the clinging attachments, there is a time of furious dashing forward, and there is a time of damping the fuel and stopping the boiling. Since coming to Japan this mountain priest has been making the pupils look into a koan, but when they have done this for a good time, he tells them to throw it down. The point is that many people come to success if they first have the experience of wrestling with a koan and later reduce the effort, but few come to success at the time when they are putting out exceptional effort. So the instruction is that those who have not yet looked into a koan absolutely must do so, but those who have had one for a good time must throw it down. At the time of zazen they throw it all away. They sleep when it is time to sleep, go when it is time to go, sit when it is time to sit, and so on as if they were not doing Zen at all. Taking things easily and without forcing, after some time the rush of thought, outward and inward, subsides naturally, and the true face shows itself as the solution to the koan without any labouring to see it. Now body and mind, free from all motivations, always appear as void and absolute sameness, shining like the brightness of heaven, at the centre of the vast expanse of phenomenal things, and needing no polishing or cleaning. This is beyond all concepts, beyond being and non-being.

Leave your innumerable knowings and seeings and under-standings, and go to that greatness of space. When you come to that vastness, there is no speck of Buddhism in your heart, and when there is no speck of knowledge about you, you will have the true sight of Buddhas and patriarchs. The true nature is like the immensity of space which contains all things. When you can go and come in all regions equally, when there is nothing specially yours, no within and no without, when you conform to high and conform to low, conform to the square and conform to the round, that is it. The emptiness of the sea allows waves to rise, the emptiness of the mountain valley makes the voice echo, the emptiness of the heart makes the Buddha. When you empty the heart, things appear as in a mirror, shining there without differences between them. Life and death an illusion, all the Buddhas one's own body.

Zen is not something mysterious; it is just hitting and piercing through. If you cut off all doubts, the course of life-and-death is cut off naturally. I ask you all: Do you see it or don't you? how in June the snow melts from the top of Mount Fuji.

Two one-minute sermons by Bukko

The dharma is different from seeing, hearing, perceiving, knowing – seeing, hearing, perceiving, knowing are all dharma.

This mountain priest makes a home for the people of the wide earth; without the dust being raised, they enter the realm of Paradise.

Lifting high his staff, he said:

Om, Om, Om! haste, haste, haste! quick, quick, quick!
bow (as you enter), bow, bow!

Throwing high, not reaching the sky;

Laying down, not reaching the earth.

All the Buddhas and patriarchs find no hold at all.

Hold, no hold.

Om! Soro, soro, shiri, shiri – divine streams rushing, rushing!
(This was a mantra of the Rig Veda adopted into Buddhism.)

Part Three
The Kamakura Koans

The collection of Japanese 'on-the-instant' koans, called Shonankattoroku, is almost unknown even to specialists. It is a record of Zen interviews given to lay pupils, from the very beginning of Zen in Japan in the thirteenth century up to the sixteenth century. The text has survived only by a series of unusual circumstances, set out briefly in a previous section and given in detail in two of the appendices to this book. There is a brief reference to it in Hayashi's *History of the Japanese Zen Sects* (1938), where two of the stories are quoted, with Imai Fukuzan's booklet as the source. In a collection of Zen stories published in 1951, the head of Kenninji temple included one story, amending the old-fashioned Japanese in places, and including the sassho test which Imai had put to the story. So Imai must have been the source here also. In the note to No. 92 (p. 159) I have mentioned that Hakuin adopted it almost word for word in two of his works, but whether he took it from a copy of the Kamakura record, or from some common source, would be for historians to determine. (I should like to thank Professor Takeji Tamamura for giving me the benefit of his vast experience in the field of Zen records.)

A number of the Kamakura koans refer to the Heart Sutra, so I have included a translation of it at the beginning, together with the 'test'. Where one of the stories depends on some background knowledge, I have inserted a note – for instance, No. 18 (p. 127) requires a knowledge of the interviews between Bukko and Tokimune. A few of Imai's notes are also included for interest.

The Zen shout rendered here as 'Katzu!' actually sounds like 'Ka...!' – the vowel is prolonged and then broken off short by a final jerk of the abdominal muscles. There is a relation to the shout given by fencers, archers and others, but that is generally Ei! or Yaaa! It too is made with a contraction of the abdominal muscles, and one of its purposes is to centre attention on the point below the navel, which helps the body to act as a unity. The Zen shout is not the same thing, and it has various purposes. One of them is to give the mind of the disciple a shake; another is simply an expression of the flood of life, like a lion's roar.

The Heart Sutra

The Heart Sutra is frequently referred to in Zen Buddhism; in some monasteries it is recited at every meal, and the monks are expected to know it by heart. There are some minor variations, but the Sutra consists of a little over two hundred Chinese characters, each of which is a monosyllable. Here is a translation which follows the commentary of a well-known Zen master of this century, Obora Ryoun.

'When the Bodhisattva Kannon was practising the profound Prajna Paramita wisdom he saw all the five aggregates to be Emptiness, and passed beyond suffering.

O disciple Shariputra, form is not different from Emptiness, Emptiness is not different from form; form is Emptiness and Emptiness is form; and so also with sensation, thinking, impulse and consciousness. All these things, Shariputra, have the character of Emptiness, neither born nor dying, neither defiled nor pure, neither increased nor lessened.

So in Emptiness there is neither form nor sensation, thinking, impulse nor consciousness; no eye, ear, nose, tongue, body nor mind; no form, sound, smell, taste, touch nor object of mind; no element of eye, nor any of the other elements, including that of mind-consciousness; no ignorance and no extinction of ignorance, nor any of the rest, including age-and-death and extinction of age-and-death; no suffering, no origination, no stopping, no path; no wisdom and no attainment.

The Bodhisattva, since he is not gaining anything, by the Prajna Paramita has his heart free from the net of hindrances, and with no hindrances in the heart there is no fear. Far from all perverted dream thoughts, he has reached ultimate Nirvana. By the Prajna Paramita all the Buddhas of the three worlds have the utmost, right and perfect enlightenment.

Know then that the Prajna Paramita is the great spiritual mantra, the great radiant mantra, the supreme mantra, the peerless mantra, which removes all suffering, the true, the unfailing. The mantra of the Prajna Paramita is taught, and it is taught thus:

Gone, gone, gone beyond, altogether beyond,
Awakening, fulfilled!'

In the Shonankattoroku collection of koans, there is one on this sutra. It runs: What is the one word which contains the whole of the Heart Sutra? Say! (There is a purely philosophical doctrine that the whole of this Sutra can be summed up in the syllable A; but this would not be accepted as an answer to the koan.)

Shōnankattōroku koans

The founder of Kenchoji temple at Kamakura in the thir-teenth century was the Chinese Zen master Daikaku, who was invited there by the Shogun Tokiyori to spread Zen in the Eastern areas of Japan. Some priests and laymen of other sects were not at all pleased at this, and out of jeal-ousy spread it around that the Zen master was a spy sent to Japan by the Mongols, and gradually many people began to believe this. At the time relations with the Mongols were worsening, and the Shogun's government, misled by the campaign of rumours, transferred the teacher to Koshu. He was not at all disturbed but joyfully followed the karma which led him away. A man came to him who was a believer in repetition of mantras like the Lotus mantra and the mantra of Amida, and said, 'The Heart Sutra which is read in the Zen tradition is long and difficult to read, whereas Nichiren teaches the mantra of the Lotus which is only seven syllables, and Ippen teaches the mantra of Amida which is only six. But the Zen Sutra is much longer and it's difficult to recite.'

The teacher listened to this and said, 'What would a fol-lower of Zen want with a long text? If you want to recite the Zen scripture, do it with *one word*. It is the the six- and seven-word ones which are too long.'

Later at the Zen temple in Koshu, Master Setsu-O used to present his pupils with this story as a riddle: The One-word Sutra of Master Daikaku. He told them: 'The golden-faced teacher (the Buddha), it is said, in all his forty-nine years of preaching never uttered a single word. But our Old Buddha (Master Daikaku) declares one word to lead the people to salvation. What is that word, say! What is that one word? If you cannot find it your whole life will be spent entangled in creepers in a dark cave.' If you find it, with a leap of realisation you will fill heaven and earth.'

Those who were set this riddle over the years tried the word 'heart', and the word 'Buddha', and 'Dharma', 'God', 'mantra', but none of them hit it. When the pearly sweat runs down the body, coming and going for the interviews with the teacher, the one word will be met directly.

NO. 5 BUKKO'S SUTRA OF NO WORD

The priest of Tsurugaoka Hachiman came to the Chinese Zen master Bukko, who succeeded Daikaku, and told him the story of Daikaku's one-word sutra. He said, 'I don't ask about the six or seven syllables which the other sects recite, but what is the one word of Zen?'

The teacher said, 'Our school does not set up words; it is a special transmission outside scriptures, a truth transmitted from heart to heart. If you can penetrate through to that, your whole life will be a mantra, and your death will be a mantra. What would you be wanting with a word or half a word? The old master Daikaku went deep into the forest and put *one word* down there, and now the whole Zen world is tearing itself to pieces on the thorns, trying to find it. If the reverend one before me wishes to grasp that one word, then without opening the mouth recite the Sutra of no-word. If you fail in your awareness of the no-word, you will at once lose the one word. Lift this one word and set it above the thirty-three heavens; bury it and it is at the bottom of the eighth great hell. The four directions and above and below, where could it be hidden? At this instant before your reverence! Is there a word, or is there not?' The golden needle did not penetrate (the embroidered cloth), and the priest silently took his leave.

NO. 6 DAIKAKU'S ONE-ROBE ZEN

A priest from the headquarters of the regent Yasutoki visited Kenchoji and remarked to Daikaku, 'Eisai and Gyoyu began the propagation of Zen here in Kamakura, but the two greatest teachers of the way of the patriarchs have been Dogen of the Soto sect and Shoichi. Both of them came to Kamakura at the invitation of regent Tokiyori to teach Zen, but both of them left before a year was out. So there are not many among the warriors here who have much understanding of Zen. In fact some are so ignorant about it that they think the character for Zen – written as they think it is by combining the characters for "garment" and "single" – means just that. They believe that Zen monks of India in the mountains practised special austerities, and even in winter wore only one cotton robe, and that the name of the sect arose from this.'

Zen   *'one-robe'*

Daikaku listened to all this and laughed. 'The people of Kamakura are right to say that Zen means wearing a single garment. They well understand what the sect stands for. An ordinary man is clad in layers of the three poisons and five desires, and though by repetition of the Buddha-name and reading the scriptures he tries again and again to strip them off, he cannot get out of his layers of passions. Fundamentally Zen means having no layers of clothes but just one piece. Repeating the Buddha-name – it is becoming just one piece with the Buddha; reading the scriptures – it is "apart from the Law no I, and without I no Law", so that I and the Law are one piece. This is called "knocking everything into one". The warriors of Kamakura, when they say Zen means the sect of a single robe, have grasped its deepest essence.

If you don't have those layers of clothes, you will be cultivating the field of the elixir (tanden) in the Zen way. Here and now let a man strip off the eighty thousand robes of the Treasure of the Law and experience the simplicity of the one robe. How would that be?'

The priest bowed in reverence and left.

Tests: Try stripping off the layers of clothes sewn during beginningless ages.

After the eighty thousand robes of the Treasure of the

Law have been stripped off, what is the single garment that remains? Speak!

One cannot go naked in the street; try wearing the single robe.

Set aside the becoming one piece with the Buddha, and try here and now becoming one with the teacher.

This began to be used as a koan in interviews at Kenchoji after Kosen, the 38th master.

BUKKO'S LOIN-CLOTH ZEN

On the staff of Yasutsura Genbansuke, a minister of the Regent Hojo Yasutoki, was one Morikatsu who happened to come to Enkakuji. There he met one of Bukko's attendants named Isshin (the compiler of the Bukkoroku records of Bukko's sermons). He said to him, 'That stupid crowd at Kamakura don't know how to write the name of your sect with the proper character (p. 19), but get it mixed up with the character for 'loin-cloth'. They're an odd lot.' The attendant was distressed that people should thus casually degrade the word Zen, and he told the teacher, who laughed and said,

'Loin-cloth is indeed the great concern of our gate, and those Kamakura soldiers must not be condemned for lack of learning. What gives the life to men is the power of the front gate, and when they die, it ends with the [excretion at the] back gate. Is not this life-and-death the great concern of our Zen gate? And what embraces the organs of life and death is the loin-cloth. If you go deep into what embraces both, you will know where life comes from and where death goes to.

Now use the loin-cloth to show our teaching to that little bit of an idiot, and make him find out how it is to destroy the loin-cloth.'

Isshin went and brandished a loin-cloth before Morikatsu's face, saying, 'All living beings are wriggling about within the loin-cloth; when you destroy the loin-cloth how is it?' Morikatsu had no words.

Test: Bring a word for Morikatsu.

This began to be used as a koan in Kamakura Zen with Kosen, the 38th Master at Kenchoji.

NO. 7 THE BUCKET WITHOUT A BOTTOM

[The nun Muchaku, whose lay name was Chiyono, was a woman of Akita who married and had one daughter. In 1277 when she was thirty-four her husband died, and she could not get over the grief. She became a nun and trained under Bukko. The story is that on the evening of the fifteenth day of August, when she was filling her lacquer flower-bucket where the valley stream comes down, the bottom fell out; seeing the water spilling she had a flash of insight and made a poem to present to the teacher.

Later the teacher set her the classical koan 'Three Gates of Oryu' and examined her minutely on it, and she was able to meet the questions. Again she had interviews for a long time, and in the end he passed over the robe and bowl' (authorised her as a successor to teach). The Uesugi family built a temple in Kyoto and proposed that she should become the first teacher there. The nun, conforming to the thing-as-it-happened within Zen, accepted.

Since the time of the Empress Danrin in the ninth century there have been many in Japan who practised Zen in the body of a woman, but Chiyono is thought to have been the first who becoming a nun received the full approval of a teacher in the line of the Zen of the Sixth Patriarch.]

Muchaku, whose lay name was Chiyono, came to Master Bukko and said, 'What is Zen?'

The teacher said, 'The heart of the one who asks is Zen: it is not to be got from the words of another.'

The nun said, 'Then what is the teacher doing, that he gives sermons and they are recorded?'

[Bukko's sermons in Sung Dynasty Chinese were recorded and afterwards translated and distributed to priests and laymen.]

The teacher said, 'With a deaf man, you show the moon by pointing; with a blind man, you show where the gate is by knocking on it with a bit of tile.'

At that moment one of the deer near the Hakugendo stream gave a cry. The teacher said, 'Where is that deer?'

The nun listened. The teacher gave a Katzu! shout and said, 'Who is this listening?'

The nun at once went out in deep reflection, and at the water-pipe from the Hakugendo she took up a lacquered wooden bucket for flowers. As she was holding it full of water, she saw the moon's reflection in it and made a poem, which was presented to the teacher:

The flower bucket took the stream water and held it,
And the reflection of the moon through the pines lodged
there in purity.

Bukko could not understand a poem in Japanese, so [his
disciple] Gio translated by rewriting it in Chinese and presented it to Bukko, who glanced at it and said, 'Nun, take the
Heart Sutra and go.'

After that, she had interviews with the master, coming
and being sent away, till in the end the lacquer bucket broke,
and she presented another poem of this realisation:

The bottom fell out of the bucket carried by Chiyono;
Now it holds no water, nor does the moon lodge there.

[In the account in Zenmonkaikiden the version is:

Chance or design? The bottom fell out of her bucket;
Now it holds no water, nor does the moon lodge there.]

After Chiyono's death the nun Nyozen of Tokeiji used to
meditate on this poem as her theme for realisation. Nyozen's
lay name was Takihime [or Takino according to the account
in the Bukedoshinshu], and she had been the wife of Oi
Toshiharu, a retainer of the Uesugi family. She trained under
Gen-o, the founder of Kaizoji temple, and in 1513 she grasped
the essence of Zen, presenting this poem to her teacher:

The bottom fell out of the bucket of that woman of humble
birth;

The pale moon of dawn is caught in the rain-puddles.

Tests: Explain plainly the song about the water from the water-pipe caught in the bucket.

Say plainly what is the bucket without a bottom.

Say plainly the meaning of the song of the nun Nyozen.

These poems were used as koans at Enkakuji temple itself after Daikyo, the fifth teacher, early in the fourteenth century. At the end of the sixteenth century 'Heart-Sutra Zen' became fashionable in Kamakura; a 'comment' had to be found to fit certain phrases of the Sutra. The poems of the two nuns came to be used as comments, so a further test came into existence:

What are the phrases from the Heart Sutra to fit the poems of the nuns? Say!

NO. 9 JIZO COMING OUT OF THE HALL

When Nitta Sadayoshi's soldiers were burning the countryside in 1331, they attacked the Kamakura temples with fire, and Kenchoji was set alight by them. It is said that the monk in charge of the main hall put the great image of Jizo on his back and carried it out of danger. The Jizo was sixteen foot in height and breadth, and weighed over 800 pounds. The doors of the Buddha-hall made an opening of only eight foot. How did the monk carry the Jizo out through that opening?

Tests: Surely here there is a man of mighty strength. Now try and see! Carry on your back an eight-hundred pound Jizo.

How do you bear out a sixteen-foot image through an eight-foot opening, Say!

This began to be used as a koan at the interviews of Master Ichigen, the 115th teacher at Kenchoji.

NO. 15 THE DRAGON CREST

During a break in the gardening, some of the gardener monks were talking under the pines in the garden behind the abbot's quarters, and it was recalled how in the old days Hojo Tokimasa [1138–1215; regent 1203–5] as a young man went into retreat at a temple on Enoshima Island, praying for lasting success in his campaigns. On the last night of the twenty-one days' retreat, a beautiful princess in a green robe appeared and prophesied, 'Your line will have the supremacy; the tide of glory is rising to your gate.' She changed into a twenty-foot snake and entered the sea, leaving three fish-like scales on the shore, which Tokimasa took and made into a luminous banner. And so it is said that the great temples of Kenchoji, Enkakuji and others have three fish-scales in their temple crests. Then the monks were arguing about the dragon carved on the pillar of one of the Enkakuji halls, and how it did not have the dragon scales in triangles like the temple crest, and some said that therefore Benzaiten (goddess of wisdom) could not have been a real dragon, and so the talk went round and round.

Master Bukko overheard this, and came and said, 'Leave the question of the three scales for a moment, but have any of you in fact seen a dragon?'

The head gardener said, 'No, I have never yet met one to see it.'

The teacher said, 'Then if you have never seen a dragon, how can you argue about how its scales ought to be? You are just like those of other sects who criticise the Buddha-heart sect without ever having had a glimpse of the Buddha heart. If you want to know how the scales ought to be, go to Enoshima for a retreat and pray to the dragon and see one. And you don't need to travel elsewhere or make any long journey. The real Benzaiten is on the crown of everyone's head. Make a meditation retreat here in the Enkakuji meditation hall for twenty-one days. If you are wholly one-pointed you will be able to see a dragon on the last day. If you can't see it on the twenty-first day, practise for twenty-one weeks. And if you still cannot see it, then press your practice on for twenty-one years, all hours of the day and night, never forgetting your resolution, and when the last day comes you will surely meet and see a dragon.'

Tests: Using the divine powers of the Way, manifest the snake body and the woman form.

How is it when you meet the dragon?

Show the scales before my eyes.

This first became a koan at the interviews of master Daisetsu, the 40th master of Enkakuji. Originally, a monk wishing to enter Enkakuji had to sit in meditation continuously for twenty-one days in accordance with this tradition, but after 1375 it was reduced to seven days.

TOKIMUNE

[Tokimune was regent of Japan from 1268 to 1284, taking up the absolute power at the age of eighteen. He was a brilliant youth but troubled with inner fears and anxieties; Tokimune entered Zen initially in the hope of getting rid of them. He practised one of the classical Zen koans but without success. When Bukko came to Japan Tokimune began to train under him; Bukko brought him to the final realisation by the shi-kin-Zen method.

There is a book attributed to Tokimune called 'Grass of the Way' which gives accounts of a number of interviews between them. In spite of some doubts as to the authorship, it is likely that some of the interviews are accurately reported. This is one of them.]

Tokimune: Of all the ills of life, fear is the worst. How can I be free from it?

Bukko: You must shut off the place where it comes from.

Tokimune: Where does fear come from?

Bukko: It comes from Tokimune.

Tokimune: Tokimune hates fear so much. How can you say it comes from Tokimune?

Bukko: Try and see. Abandon Tokimune and come tomorrow: your courage will be as great as the whole world.

Tokimune: How do I abandon Tokimune?

Zen Master Daikaku,
founder of Kenchoji temple at Kamakura.
(Kamakura Museum)

Bukko: You must simply cut off all thinking.

Tokimune: What is the way to cut off all thinking?

Bukko: Plunge yourself into meditation, and wait for the body and mind to become serene.

Tokimune: My duties in the world leave me so little time. What can I do?

Bukko: … Going and sitting and staying and lying, whatever you have to do, that itself is the best place of practice [dojo] for training. That is the place to learn profound meditation.

The teacher Bukko further gave Tokimune five rules:

(1) Try hard to keep your mind set at the Field of Elixir [tanden] just below the navel. Keep yourself always calm like pure water and don't be anxious about things.

(2) Don't clutch after any outer thing. Remain in the state 'I alone am the Honoured One' [declaration of Buddha at birth].

(3) Don't labour to check thinking. But neither is thinking to be left unchecked. Just see to it that no thought is born.

(4) Always keep a spirit of daring, a daring spirit that does not hesitate to tread on a sword.

(5) If your vision is narrow, your courage also will be narrow. Always try to keep your thoughts universal.

[During almost the whole of Tokimune's rule, the threat of Mongol invasion hung over Japan. When the threat became acute, Tokimune visited the teacher who gave him the three Chinese characters, read in Japanese Maku-mo-zo, 'No delusive thoughts!' The teacher said, 'This spring and summer there will be great fighting at Hakata where they will seek to land, but have no anxiety about it. No delusive thoughts, no delusive thoughts! No hesitation in yourself, no indecision, and then what cause for grief anywhere?'

That year in May the Mongol armada sailed for Japan, and when the news came, Tokimune in armour went to see the teacher: 'The great thing has come', to which the teacher replied, 'Can you somehow avoid it?'

Tokimune calmly stamped his feet, shook his whole body and gave a tremendous shout of Katzu!

The teacher said, 'A real lion cub, a real lion roar. Dash straight forward and don't look round!'

After the defeat of the Mongols, Tokimune built the great monastery of Enkakuji at Kamakura, and installed in it the representation of Jizo-of-a-Thousand-Forms. Bukko became the first teacher there. Tokimune organised a great service for the souls of the dead of both sides.

Soon afterwards he died at the age of thirty-three. In the funeral oration Bukko said that he had been a Bodhisattva – 'for nearly twenty years he ruled without showing joy or anger; when the victory came he showed no elation; he sought for the truth of Zen and found it.']

NO. 18 TOKIMUNE'S THING BELOW THE NAVEL

When Tokimune at the outbreak of hostilities visited Bukko, he gave the Katzu! shout of dashing straight forward. The shout was so great that it echoed from Deer Mountain. Priest Gio said, 'The general has something great below the navel, so the shout too is great.'

[In Taoist teaching in Sung China there was a focus of spiritual vitality just below the navel. It was formally called the Field of Elixir (tanden) in the Sea of Life (kikai), and the point for concentration was about an inch below the navel. In Szechuan dialect it was colloquially referred to as 'thing below the navel'. Gio was a priest from Szechuan who had come with Daikaku to Japan, and in praising Tokimune's tanden he used this slang phrase about the greatness of the thing below the navel. It was transcribed into phonetic Japanese as 'shii ku ii mo', and later written in Chinese characters, which Japanese would read as 'sai ka ichi motsu', meaning one thing below the navel. The Japanese did not know the Szechuan phrase and took it in another meaning.

The courtier Masanori, when he understood what Gio had said, asked him, 'When did Your Reverence see the size of what the general has below his navel?'

The priest said, 'Before the general was born, I saw it.'

The courtier did not understand.

The priest said, 'If you do not understand the greatness of what is below the general's navel, then see through to before you yourself were born, the greatness of the thing below the navel. How would that thing become greater or less by the honour or contempt of high or low?

The courtier was still more bewildered.

The priest gave a Katzu! shout and said, 'Such is the voice of it, of that thing.'

At these words the courtier had an insight and said, 'This petty official today has been fortunate enough to receive a Katzu! from you. I have known the greatness of that thing below our lord's navel.'

The priest said, 'What is its length and breadth, say!'

The courtier said, 'Its length pierces the three worlds: its breadth pervades all ten directions.'

The priest said, 'Let the noble officer present a Katzu! of that greatness to show the proof.'

The courtier was not able to open his mouth.

Tests: What is the meaning of dashing straight ahead?

Say directly, what is the general's dashing straight forward.

Leaving the general's dashing straight forward, what is your dashing straight forward, here and now? Speak!

Leaving your dashing straight forward, what is the dashing straight forward of all the Buddhas and beings of the three worlds?

Leaving the dashing straight forward of the Buddhas and beings, what is the dashing straight forward of heaven and earth and the ten thousand phenomena?

Leaving for the moment the thing below the navel of the Taoists, what is the thing below the navel in our tradition? Say!

Say something about the thing below the navel before father and mother were born.

When the light of life has failed, then say something of that thing below the navel.

Leaving the general's Katzu! – when you yourself are threatened by an enemy from somewhere, what great deed will you perform? Say!

Give a Katzu! for the courtier to prove it.

This became a koan when Torin, 44th master of Kenchoji, began to use it in interviews.

[According to the records in Gosan-nyudoshu in Kamakura, the samurai there were set this koan and wrestled with it, and even after 'seeing the nature' they were never passed through it for at least five or six years. It is said that 'dash straight forward' in the first tests was often taken in the meaning of 'swiftly' or else 'sincerely' and that these were not passed.]

NO. 19 THE GATE TO THE WORLD OF ALL BUDDHAS

Originally Enkakuji was a place forbidden to women, with the exception that unmarried women of a samurai family who were training at Zen were allowed to come and go through the gate. After 1334 a rule was made that unless a woman had attained 'seeing the nature' she was not allowed to go up to the Great Light Hall. In time it became the custom that the keeper of the gate, when a woman applied to go through, would present a test question. According to one Zen tradition from that time, five tests were in use at the gate of Enkakuji:

The gate has many thresholds: even Buddhas and patriarchs cannot get through.

If you would enter, give the pass-word.

The strong iron door is hardly to be opened.
Let one of mighty power tear it off its hinges.

Vast outstretched in all directions — no door, no gate.
How will you recognise the gate?

84,000 gates open at the same time.
He whose eye is single, let him see.

What is it? this gate by which
All the Buddhas come into the world.

The gate of Enkakuji.
(International Society for Educational
Information, Tokyo)

[Tokeiji was a training temple for women, of which the first teacher was the nun Shido, widow of Tokimune. There was a tradition that Shido had her realisation when meditating before a mirror; following the tradition of the founder, there was a mirror over six foot in diameter hanging in the meditation hall at Tokeiji. Part of the training of the nuns was to polish it and meditate facing it. Each of the successive teachers wrote a Japanese poem on the subject of the mirror, and these poems finally became koans for the nuns and others. When a nun began to attain samadhi on the poem, the teacher would put certain 'tests' which had to be answered out of samadhi-experience and not by quotation. It was sometimes required to give a 'chakugo' or Zen comment; at Tokeiji this was often an individual expression, but it was also allowed to quote from Zen classics, if the nun knew any phrase from one which seemed to her to express her experience. Towards the end of the sixteenth century, quotations from the Zenrinkushu anthology of Zen phrases became more and more frequent. In later centuries it became necessary to find one specific phrase in order to be passed through each test.

As an example, here are the first eight poems composed on the mirror by the first eight teachers at Tokeiji; these were presented as koans to the nuns, and some of the replies recorded by the nun Myoto from interviews in the year 1596 are here added, from the records of Tokeiji. The master was Sanpaku, the 156th teacher of Enkakuji. He did not necessarily pass all these 'comments' and answers.]

(1) The poem of the founder, the nun Shido:

If the mind does not rest on anything, there is no
clouding
And talk of polishing is but a fancy.

Test: If the mind does not rest on anything, then how will
things be seen or heard or known or understood?
Comment: Rising and sinking according to the current,
Going and coming, no footprint remains.

Test: A mirror which does not cloud and needs no polishing –
    Set it before the teacher now.

The nun meditating on the mirror.
(Morikawa)

(2) The poem of the second teacher, the nun Runkai:
   Various the reflections, yet its surface is unscarred;
   From the very beginning unclouded, the pure mirror.

Test: When it reflects variously, how is it then?
Comment: The mind turns in accordance with the ten thousand things;
   The pivot on which it turns is verily in the depths.

Test: From the very beginning the mirror unclouded:
How then are there reflections of Karmic obstacles in it?
Comment: Within the pure mirror never clashing against each other,
   The reflections of pine and bamboo in harmony.

Test: Show the pure mirror right before the teacher's face.
Comment: Heaven and earth one clear mirror,
   Now as of old, luminous and majestic.

(3) The poem of the third teacher, Shotaku:

   As night falls, no more reflections in the mirror,
   Yet in this heart they are darkly seen.

Comment: In the dark night, things in front of the mirror are seen no more by the eye, yet images are reflected in the heart, and in face of them we go astray. When we have passed beyond this path of illusion, then our gaze pierces through even the darkest night to see the sun-Buddha ever shining everywhere, illumining all.

Test: What is the colour and shape of that heart which sees in the dark?

(4) The poem of the fourth teacher, Junso:

> Reflections are clear yet do not touch the eye,
> And the I facing the mirror is also forgotten.

Test: If you think the reflections are there but do not touch the eye, this is already a dust on the mirror; then what is the meaning?

Try and see!

Comment: When it is said that they do not touch the eye, it means that the eye is not joined to awareness; there is no agitation in the heart. So there is not even the thought that they do not touch the eye.

Test: What is the state of the mirror when the I has been forgotten?

[To this test the nun had to demonstrate directly without recourse to words.]

Test: What is the difference between forgetting-I Zen and Void Zen (Ku-zen)?

Comment: Aspiring to heaven but not seeing heaven;
Searching for earth but not seeing earth.

(5) Poem of the fifth teacher, the former princess Yodo:
Heart unclouded, heart clouded;
Rising and falling are yet the same body.

Test: Heart unclouded, what is that?
Comment: Ten thousand miles without a cloud, ten thousand miles of heaven.

Test: Heart clouded, how is that?
Comment: In spring clouds rise round the mountain
    And in the cave it is dark.

Test: Rising and falling, how is that?
Comment: The moon sets, and in the pool no reflection;
    A cloud is born and the mountain has a robe.

(6) Poem of the sixth teacher, Ninbo:

    Even when there is no mirror to reflect the things
    Every time one looks, there is a mirror reflecting them in the heart.

Test: What is this looking?
Test: What is this reflecting heart?

    [To these tests the nun had to demonstrate directly without recourse to words.]

(7) Poem of the seventh teacher Ryodo:
    If you ask how it is that the reflections in the pure mirror die away and perish,
    You will come to know where they really are.
Test: Right now the teacher asks, where are the reflections? Answer well! Where are they?

Comment: Shut the door and push out the moon:
Dig a well and chisel space apart.

(8) Poem of the eighth teacher, the nun Kanso:
    Clouded over from beginningless ages is the pure mirror:
    when polished, it reflects – the holy form of Amida.

Test: What is this polishing? Speak!
Test: Declare the form of Amida.
After this second test had been passed, a suitable comment
had to be supplied. One of them was:
    This body the Lotus Paradise, this heart indeed Amida.

[There is a record of one of the training retreats at Tokeiji
in 1596 attended by 108 nuns. Forty-six of them who were
taking Kamakura Zen koans composed their own comments.
The teacher did not pass all of them. There were 17 nuns who
were at the stage of having to submit comments on the classical Chinese koans, and 8 of these composed Japanese-style
poems for the occasion; the others presented phrases from
the Zenrinkushu anthology.

Thirty-five of the nuns were passed through their koans.
The nun Myotei distinguished herself by passing the notori-
ously difficult koan called the 'Four Katzu! shouts of Master
Rinzai'. The details of all the koan answers and comments at this training session were recorded but kept as
secret records.]

*Polishing and the Buddha appearing
in the mirror. (Morikawa)*

ZEN AND THE WAYS

The Shogun Yoriie detested the followers of the Nembutsu [recitation of the name of Amida Buddha in the formula Na-mu-A-mi-da-butsu], and in May 1213 he issued a decree forbidding the recitation. He ordered Yashiro Hiki to investigate travellers, and if he found any priest of the Nembutsu persuasion, to take his robe and burn it. To carry out this order, Yashiro inspected travellers at the side of Mandokoro bridge, and if he found any priest of Nembutsu, he stripped off his robe and burnt it. If he discovered he was breaking the decree banning Nembutsu, he arrested him and threw him into prison.

At this time there was in Ise a Nembutsu follower called Shonenbo [the Name-reciting priest], and he came to Kamakura and performed the recitation there. Yashiro arrested him and went to burn his robe. Shonenbo said, 'This robe is the banner of the Three Treasures, it is the holy sign of the sangha, it is the garment of the shadow of all the Buddhas. It is the dress of honour of the Four Guardian Kings and the Eight Dragons. And especially a robe of shonen [recitation], if it has been an expression of great faith, will not burn even when thrown into a fire.' Yashiro then told his men to throw the robe into a blazing fire. Shonenbo gave one cry of Namu-Amidabutsu, and the fire went out without burning even the edge of the robe – so it is related.

The priest Sonei approached Master Nanzan with this story, and the teacher said to him, 'Leave this little tale which the followers of the Kamakura Pure Land sect have passed down. Right now before you, when the robe-body is thrown into the fire, how can Shonenbo save himself?

Try a Nembutsu recitation! Prove it to this old teacher.'
  Sonei had no words.

Test: In the blazing fire, how can he save himself? Say something for Sonei.

This became a koan in Kamakura at the interviews of Yuho, the 30th master of Zenkoji temple.

NO. 31 THE VERY FIRST JIZO

Sakawa Koresada, a direct retainer of the Uesugi family, entered the main hall at Kenchoji and prayed to the Jizo-of-a-Thousand-Forms there. Then he asked the attendant monk in charge of the hall:
  'Of these thousand forms of Jizo, which is the very first Jizo?'
  The attendant said, 'In the breast of the retainer before me are a thousand thoughts and ten thousand imaginings; which of these is the very first one?'
  The samurai was silent.
  The attendant said again, 'Of the thousand forms of Jizo, the very first Jizo is the Buddha-lord who is always using those thousand forms.'
  The warrior said, 'Who is this Buddha-lord?'
  The attendant suddenly caught him and twisted his nose. The samurai immediately had a realisation.

Tests: Which is the very first Jizo out of the thousand-formed Jizo?

Which is the very first out of the thousand thoughts and ten thousand imaginings?

What did Koresada realise when his nose was twisted?

This became a koan at the interviews of koken, the 61st master at Kenchoji.

As the torrent of water can have no effect on the tremendous strength of the tiger, which in fact enjoys it, so the torrents of worldly hostility, or temptation, have no effect on the inner serenity of Zen. (Kamakura Museum)

The nun Myoan of Tokeiji practised Zen in interviews with Tanei, the 74th teacher at Enkakuji, who set her as koans the poems composed by Yodo (fifth abbess of Tokeiji and a former princess) and her attendants. These poems were on the theme of gathering and arranging the flowers on the birthday of Buddha. The poem of Yodo is:

Decorate the heart of the beholder,
For the Buddha of the flower hall
Is nowhere else.

The Buddha-nature as a baby.
(Kamakura Museum)

Tests: By what do you recognise the heart of the beholder?
Say how you would decorate the flower hall.

If it is to worship a Buddha who is nowhere else than in the heart, what do you want with a flower hall? Say!

The poem of Ika, a former court lady, is:

Throw away into the street the years of the past.
What is born now on the flower dais,
Let it raise its new-born cry.

Tests: When the years have been thrown away into the street, what is it that is born in their place?
Let the teacher here and now listen to the new-born cry.
Where is the flower dais?

The poem of the nun Myoko is:

Born, and forgetting the parents who bore it –
The parents who are Shaka and Amida.

Tests: What does the poem mean?
Where is the birth?
Where are Shaka and Amida?
Speak a word of when parents and child come face to face.

The poem of the nun Atoku, another of the attendants, is:
Coming out from the Buddha-womb
to become myself,
Now let it ring out – the Dharma's new-born cry.

Tests: What is it like in the Buddha-womb?
Let the Dharma's new-born cry ring out.

[The teacher Tanei used these poems of Yodo and the attendants, sung by them on the birthday festival on 8 April, as koans for the nuns of Tokeiji. And in the Kamakura temples, these and other koans on everyday things were given first, instead of classical Chinese koans, to novice and nuns who had scanty literary attainments.]

NO. 42 SERMON

The head monk at Hokokuji temple was deaf and could not hear the preaching of the Dharma. He asked to take charge of the sutras as librarian, and for more than ten years he perused them. But he found that the accounts of the Buddha's life in the various sutras did not agree, and he asked Abbot Hakudo, the fifth master of the temple, which was right. The Abbot said, 'What is in the sutras is as a finger pointing to the moon or a net to catch fish. What is a Zen man doing muddying his mind with sutra-phrases and inferences about various teachings and wanting to know which is right and which is wrong? The head monk's practice is itself the Buddha's practice; when the head monk left home that was itself the Buddha's leaving home. When the head monk attained the Way, that was itself the Buddha's attaining the Way. When the head monk enters Nirvana, that is the Buddha entering Nirvana. The head monk has already left home and is far advanced in the Way, but has not yet entered Nirvana;

he is today in the stage of the forty-nine years of preaching. Now, for the sake of men and heaven and the ten thousand beings, let him try giving a sermon. Attention all!'

The koan: Say what sermon it is that the great ones of the Sangha give as their sermon for men and heaven!

Tests: You are giving your sermon in the high heaven-world, and now you rise to the world of no form. To that which has no colour or form, what is your sermon? Say!

In heaven when you are told to face the Brahma-king, how do you make your sermon? Say!

You rise to the skies and come to the heaven of Maitreya and enter the palace of Maitreya – how will be your sermon? Say!

You go to the heaven on Meru, and you are invited to take the Dharma-seat of Jizo. How will you make your sermon? Say!

You enter the dragon palace in the ocean. For the eight Dragon Kings, how will be your sermon? Say!

A man comes and asks you to give a sermon to a baby less than a month old. How do you make the sermon? Say!

There is a deaf old man of over a hundred. You are asked to give a sermon, but he cannot hear anything of the teaching because of his deafness. To this deaf man, how do you make the sermon? Say!

There is a furious brigand, who as yet has no belief in the Three Treasures of Buddhism, and in the middle of the night he comes to your room, waves a naked sword over your head and demands money. If you have nothing to give him, your life will be cut off by his sword. For this man what will your sermon be? Say!

A foreign enemy invades our country, killing and plundering. When this man comes and you are asked to give him the Sermon For The Brigand, you do not know his foreign language. At this moment what will you do to make your sermon? Say!

You are face to face with death, your life is running out, you can hardly breathe and cannot open your mouth. Then a man asks you for a sermon on entering Nirvana. By what means do you make your sermon? Say!

You enter hell. When you preach a sermon for Emma-O the judge of the dead, how will you teach then? Say!

The beings in hell are night and day screaming in pain and have no time to hear the teaching. To those on the sword-mountain, to those in the blood-lake, how will you give a sermon? Say!

You are born in the paradise of the Pure Land. With what sermon will you glorify the holy teachings of Amida? Say!

When you are asked to give the sermons of the Buddha's forty-nine years preaching in one word, how will your sermon be? Say!

The main koan began to be used as such in Kamakura Zen with the 13th master of Hokokuji temple. When he put his disciples under the hammer with this koan, he always made them go through all the fifteen questions, and in the Bukedoshin records they are called the Fifteen Gates of Hokokuji.

A doctor attached to the Bakufu government put up a notice at the great gate of Hokokuji which said:

Though you pass the five gates of Hokokuji, there are fifteen gates still to pass in the Master's interview room.

The Sorin-zakki miscellaneous records state that when young monks came to Hokokuji seeking lodging for a night, they were first presented with these fifteen questions, and if they could meet one of them properly, they were allowed to stay.

NO. 44 WIELDING THE SPEAR WITH HANDS EMPTY

[Nanjio Masatomo, a master of the spear, was at Kenchoji to worship, and afterwards spoke with priest Gio about using a spear on horseback. Gio said, 'Your Honour is indeed well versed in the art of the spear. But until you have known the state of wielding the spear with hands empty, you will not penetrate to the ultimate secret of the art.' Nanjio said, 'What do you mean?' The teacher said, 'No spear in the hands, no hands on the spear.' The spear master did not understand. The teacher said further, 'If you don't understand, your art of the spear is a little affair of the hands alone.']

In December of 1256 Fukuzumi Hideomi, a government official, was given the koan 'wielding the spear with hands empty'. He wrestled furiously with this without being able to attain the state, and one evening he paced to and fro many times between the outer hall of Kenchoji and the approach to the teacher's room, until he was exhausted. He quietly crept into a little grotto near the hall, and repeated again and again 'empty hands, empty hands (kara-te, kara-te)'. However a monk who was doing a punishment sitting (to sit all night in meditation posture for having broken a monastery rule) overheard

Hideomi when in his meditation he said 'kara-te, kara-te', and thought it was 'kane-dase, kane-dase (give some money, give some money)'. He thought it was a robber and raised the alarm. The priest with the office of jikijitsu and others made a quick search round the hall, and caught Hideomi.

At that time Hideomi was very ill with tuberculosis of the lungs, and moreover in his absorption with the koan, he had forgotten to eat for several days, so that his flesh was wasted and his bones weak, and his body on the verge of death. The jikijitsu Chiko hit him on the back and said, 'Let not this heart be *set* on any place', and gave a Katzu! shout.

Hideomi nodded, and then quietly died.

Tests: How is it, to wield a spear with hands empty?

What has the phrase about not setting the heart got to do with the empty hands koan?

This became a koan with the interviews of Kosen, the 38th teacher at Kenchoji.

NO. 52 THE NIGHT INTERVIEW OF THE NUN MYOTEI

Myotei was a widow and a woman well known for her strength of character. She trained for some years under Kimon, the 150th Master of Enkakuji; on a chance visit to the temple she had had an experience while listening to a sermon by him on the Diamond Sutra. In the year 1568 she took part in the Rohatsu training week. [This is the most severe training week of the year; it is at the beginning of December, when according to tradition the Buddha meditated six days and nights, then looked at the morning star and attained full realisation. There is almost continuous meditation broken only by interviews with the teacher, sutra chanting, meals and tea; this goes on for a week, with very little or no sleep according to the temple. On the morning after the last night's meditation and interviews the participants look together at the morning star.]

Before one of the night interviews she took off her robes and came in without anything on at all. She lay down before the teacher, who picked up his iron nyo-i [ceremonial stick) and thrust it out towards her thighs, saying, 'What trick is this?'

The nun said, 'I present the gate by which all the Buddhas of the three realms come into the world.'

The teacher said, 'Unless the Buddhas of the three realms go in, they cannot come out. Let the gate be entered here and now' and he sat astride the nun.

She demanded, 'He who should enter, what Buddha is that?'

The teacher said, 'What is to be from the beginning has no "should" about it.'

The nun said, 'He who does not give his name is a barbarian brigand, who is not allowed to enter.'

The teacher said, 'Maitreya Buddha, who has to be born to save the people after the death of Shakyamuni Buddha, enters the gate.'

The nun made as if to speak and the teacher quickly covered her mouth. He pressed the iron stick between her thighs saying, 'Maitreya Buddha enters the gate. Give birth this instant!'

The nun hesitated and the teacher said, 'This is no true womb; how could this give birth to Maitreya?'

The nun went out and at the interview the next morning the teacher said, 'Have you given birth to Maitreya?'

The nun cried with great force, 'He was born quietly last night.' She caught hold of the teacher and put her hands round the top of his head saying, 'I invite the Buddha to take the top of this head as the Lion Throne. Let him graciously preach a sermon from it.'

The teacher said, 'The way is one alone, not two, not three.'

The nun said, 'In their abilities, the beings differ in ten thousand ways. How should you stick to one way?'

The teacher said, 'One general at the head of ten thousand men enters the capital.'

Tests: What is the real meaning of Myotei's coming naked for the night interview?

The nun hesitated about giving birth to Maitreya. Say something for her.

What does the one general and the ten thousand soldiers mean? What is it directly? Now say!

This became a koan in Kamakura Zen, and after the time of the nun Ryodo, the seventh teacher at Tokeiji, was given to nuns in the whole eastern part of Japan. [If this is so, there must be a scribal error in the date at the beginning.]

In 1299 when Fukada Sadatomo came to Kenchoji for a ceremony, he met the teacher in a room where there happened to be a picture of the contemporary Sung dynasty beauty Rei Shojo. He asked Master Saikan, 'Who is that?'

The teacher replied, 'It is said it happens to be Rei Shojo.'

Sadatomo looked at the picture admiringly and remarked, 'That picture is powerfully painted and yet of the utmost delicacy. Is that woman now in the Sung country [China]?'

The teacher said, 'What do you mean, in the Sung? Now, here, in Japan.'

The noble said, 'And where is that?'

The master said loudly, 'Lord Sadatomo!' The noble looked up.

'And where is that?' said the teacher.

Sadatomo grasped the point and bowed.

Test: What did Lord Sadatomo grasp?

This became a koan at Kenchoji from the time of Do-an, the 105th master there.

NO. 68 THE GREAT KATZU! OF MASTER TODEN

Yoriyasu was a swaggering and aggressive samurai. [In the Nirayama manuscript of Bukedoshinshu and in some other accounts the name is given as Yorihara.] In the spring of 1341 he was transferred from Kofu to Kamakura, where he visited

Master Toden, the 45th teacher at Kenchoji, to ask about Zen. The teacher said, 'It is to manifest directly the Great Action in the hundred concerns of life. When it is loyalty as a samurai, it is the loyalty of Zen. "Loyalty" is written with the Chinese character made up of "centre" and "heart", so it means the lord in the centre of the man. There must be no wrong passions. But when this old priest looks at the samurai today, there are some whose heart centre leans towards name and money, and others where it is towards wine and lust, and with others it is inclined towards power and bravery. They are all on those slopes, and cannot have a centred heart; how could they have loyalty to the state? If you, Sir, wish to practise Zen, first of all practise loyalty and do not slip into wrong desires.'

The warrior said, 'Our loyalty is direct Great Action on the battlefield. What need have we for sermons from a priest?'

The teacher replied, 'You Sir are a hero in strife, I am a gentleman of peace – we can have nothing to say to each other.'

The warrior then drew his sword and said, 'Loyalty is in the hero's sword, and if you do not know *this*, you should not talk of loyalty. '

The teacher replied, 'This old priest has the treasure sword of the Diamond King, and if you do not know it, you should not talk of the source of loyalty.'

The samurai said, 'Loyalty of your Diamond Sword – what is the use of that sort of thing in actual fighting?'

The teacher jumped forward and gave one Katzu! shout, giving the samurai such a shock that he lost consciousness. After some time the teacher shouted again and the samurai at once recovered. The teacher said, 'The loyalty in the hero's sword, where is it? Speak!'

The samurai was over-awed; he apologised and took his departure.

[In the account in the sixth volume of Gosannyudoshu it is added that Yorihara wept and presented his sword in token of repentance.]

Test: Right now before you is that samurai. Try a shout that the teacher may see the proof.

This became a koan in Kamakura after Koten, the 57th Master at Kenchoji.

NO. 69 THE PAPER SWORD

In 1331 when Nitta Yoshisada was fighting against Hojo Sadatoki, a chief retainer of the Hojo family, named Sakurada Sadakuni, was slain. His wife Sawa wished to pray for the dead man; she cut off her hair and entered Tokeiji as the nun Shotaku. For many years she devoted herself to Zen under the seventeenth teacher at Enkakuji, and in the end she became the third teacher of Tokeiji. In the Rohatsu training week of December 1339, she was returning from her evening interview with the teacher at Enkakuji, when on the way a man armed with a sword saw her and was attracted by her beauty. He threatened her with the sword and came to rape her. The nun took out a piece of paper and rolled it up, then thrust it like a sword at the man's eyes. He became unable to strike and was completely overawed by her spiritual strength.

He turned to run and the nun gave a Katzu! shout, hitting him with the paper sword. He fell and then fled.

Test: Show the paper sword which is the heart sword, and prove its actual effect now.

NO. 70 HEAVEN AND EARTH BROKEN UP

Tadamasa, a senior retainer of Hojo Takatoki the Regent, had the Buddhist name Anzan (quiet mountain). He was a keen Zen follower and for twenty-three years came and went to the meditation hall for laymen at Kenchoji. When the fighting broke out everywhere in 1331, he was wounded in one engagement, but in spite of the pain galloped to Kenchoji to see Sozan, the 27th teacher there. A tea ceremony was going on at Kenchoji, and the teacher seeing the man in armour come in, quickly put a teacup in front of him and said, 'How is this?'

The warrior at once crushed it under his foot and said, 'Heaven and earth broken up altogether.'

The teacher said, 'When heaven and earth are broken up, how is it with you?'

Anzan stood with his hands crossed over his breast. The teacher hit him, and he involuntarily cried out from the pain of his wounds.

The teacher said, 'Heaven and earth not quite broken up yet.'

The drum sounded from the camp across the mountain, and Tadamasa galloped quickly back. The next evening he came again, covered with blood, to see the teacher. The teacher came out and said again,

'When heaven and earth are broken up, how is it with you?'

Anzan, supporting himself on his blood-stained sword, gave a great Katzu! and died standing in front of the teacher.

Test: When heaven and earth are broken up, how is it with you? [In the Bukedoshinshu, the version is: When the elements of the body are dispersed, where are you?]

This began to be used as a koan in the interviews of priest Jikusen, the 29th master of Kenchoji.

NO. 74 PAINTING THE NATURE

Ekichu, the seventh master of Jufukuji, was famous as a painter. One day Nobumitsu came to see him and asked whether he could paint the fragrance described in the famous line 'After walking through flowers, the horse's hoof is fragrant.' The teacher drew a horse's hoof and a butterfly fluttering round it (attracted by the fragrance).

Then Nobumitsu quoted the line 'Spring breeze over the river bank' and asked for a picture of the breeze. The teacher drew a branch of willow waving.

Nobumitsu cited the famous Zen phrase, 'A finger direct to the human heart, See the nature to be Buddha.' He asked for a picture of the heart. The teacher picked up the brush and flicked a spot of ink onto Nobumitsu's face. The warrior was surprised and annoyed, and the teacher rapidly sketched the angry face.

Then Nobumitsu asked for a picture of the 'nature' as in the phrase 'see the nature'. The teacher broke the brush and said, 'That's the picture'.

Nobumitsu did not understand and the teacher remarked, 'If you haven't got that seeing eye, you can't see it.'

Nobumitsu said, 'Take another brush and paint the picture of the nature.'

The teacher replied, 'Show me your nature and I will paint it.' Nobumitsu had no words.

Tests: How would you show the nature?

Come, see your nature and bring the proof of it.

Say something for Nobumitsu.

NO. 80 THE COPY

A head monk came to Gyokuzan, the 21st master of Kenchoji, and saluted him. He asked whether he might copy out the sermons on the Rinzairoku which had been given by Daikaku, the founder of Kenchoji.

The teacher sat silent for a good time, and then said, 'Have you copied it?'

'Why,' said the head monk, 'I have not yet had the loan of it.'

The teacher replied, 'Rinzai's Zen is communicated from heart to heart – what should you want with writings? If you have to have a writing, take Mount Ashigara as the brush and Yui shore as the ink-stone, and make your copy.

The head monk gave a Katzu! shout and said, 'I have made my copy.'

Tests: What is the writing of the founder, that it can be copied by a shout?

Try a Katzu! yourself and make proof of it.

NO. 87 THE SERMON OF NUN SHIDO

At the Rohatsu training week of 1304 at Enkakuji, Master Chokei ['Peach-tree Valley' – the fourth teacher of Enkakuji] gave his formal approval (inka) as a teacher to the nun Shido, the founder of Tokeiji. The head monk did not approve of the inka being granted, and asked a question to test her:

'In our line, one who receives the inka gives a discourse on the Rinzairoku classic. Can the nun teacher really brandish the staff of the Dharma in the Dharma-seat?'

The nun Shido.
(International Society for Educational Information, Tokyo)

She faced him and drew out the ten-inch knife (carried by all women of the warrior class) and held it up: 'Certainly a Zen teacher of the line of the patriarch should go up on the high seat and speak on the book. But I am a woman of the warrior line and I should declare our teaching when really face to face with a drawn sword. What book should I need?'

The head monk said, 'Before father and mother were born, with what then will you declare our teaching?'

The nun closed her eyes for some time. Then she said, 'Do you understand?'

The head monk said, 'A wine-gourd has been tipped right up in Peach-tree Valley; Drunken eyes see ten miles of flowers.'

Tests: Before father and mother were born, what was the sermon? Say!

Listen to the sermon of the nun Shido.

These two tests were used from the time of the 17th teacher in Enkakuji itself, but at Tokeiji two more were also added:

What is the meaning of the poem which the head monk made? Are its two lines praise or criticism?

NO. 88 THE KNIGHT PATRIARCH COMING FROM THE WEST

Yamana Morofuyu was a brave warrior of the Ashikagas, who was transferred from being a naval captain to the cavalry. For some time after that he trained in Zen at Enkakuji. One year he came to the Rohatsu training week in December, but would not sit in the special meditation hall reserved for the warriors. Instead he was riding his horse all day over the mountains. Master Daikyo, the 43rd teacher at Enkakuji, warned him against this, saying, 'On horseback your heart will easily be distracted. During the Rohatsu, sit in the hall.'

He said: 'Monks are men of Zen sitting, and should certainly do their meditation in the special Buddha place. But I am a knight and should practise my meditation on horseback.'

The teacher said, 'Your Honour was formerly a sea captain, and now become a knight. The patriarch's coming (from India to China) on the waves, and the patriarch's coming on horseback, is the meaning the same or different?'

Morofuyu hesitated.

The teacher snatched the whip and hit him with it, saying, 'Oh, ride away, ride away.'

Test: Say something for Morofuyu.

This became a koan in Kamakura Zen with the interviews of master Shuntei, the 47th teacher at Enkakuji.

NO. 92 MEDITATION OF THE ENERGY-SEA

A retired landowner named Sadashige of Awafune [the present-day Ofuna] trained at Kenchoji under Nanzan, the 20th master. Once he was away for a time and when he returned the teacher said, 'You have been ill, Sir, and for some time you have not come to the Zen sitting here. Have you now been able to purify and calm your kikai (energy-sea)?'

Sadashige said, 'Following your holy instruction I have meditated on the kikai and been able to attain purity and calm.'

The teacher said, 'Bring out what you have understood of the meditation and say something on it.'

(1) This my kikai tanden, breast, belly, [down to the] soles of the feet, [is] altogether my original face.
Test: What nostrils would there be on that face?

(2) This my kikai tanden
[is] altogether this my true home.
Test: What news would there be from the true home?

(3) This my kikai tanden
[is] altogether this my lotus paradise of consciousness-only.
Test: What pomp would there be in the lotus paradise?

(4) This my kikai tanden
[is] altogether the Amida of my own body.
Test: What sermon would that Amida be preaching?

This koan was first given in the interviews of Master Nanzan.

[In the Bushosodan record in Zenkoji these are given as four separate meditations. Centuries later, Hakuin refers to them in two works, Orategama and Yasenkanna. The version in

'Yasenkanna' is closest to the one here. The four meditations are identical except that the first one has 'loins, legs, soles of the feet', and in all four the phrase kikai tanden is preceded by the descriptive 'below the navel'. Some of the Chinese expressions are given in a simpler Japanese form. Each koan and its test run on as one sentence. In Orategama there are more changes. The phrase 'loins, legs, soles of the feet' is repeated each time, the order is changed, and there is an extra koan '... altogether this is Joshu's Mu: what is the truth of the Mu?' In this version the 'my' is omitted before 'original face'. These are small changes and it is clear that Hakuin must derive his kikai tanden method from the Kamakura text, or from a source common to both.]

NO. 100 FREEING THE GHOST

In 1293 Hirotada was taking as a koan the four phrases of the Diamond Sutra:

> If as a form he would see me
>> Or by sound or word would seek me,
> This one on the wrong path
>> cannot see the Buddha.

But he still could not see into it. He was sitting in meditation in the cave called Snow-gate, which is one of the three near the Tosotsuryo, the tomb of the founder of Kenchoji. While he was unaware of anything in his samadhi, the ground opened and the timbers and stones of the building collapsed into the fissure, burying him. That night the apparition of Hirotada was seen before the hall of the founder, repeating 'Cannot see the Buddha, cannot see the Buddha' without ceasing. The monk Kei [Mori Sokei, who had the position of jishinban] confronted the ghost and shouted one question, at which it suddenly vanished and never showed itself again.

[*Note*: In 1293 there was a great earthquake at Kamakura, during which the ground opened, bringing down buildings and killing many people. This was the occasion for the first of the great fires at Kenchoji.]

Tests: Why did the head monk have to ask the question? Say!

What is the connection between the question and the 'Cannot see the Buddha'? Say!

What did Hirotada's ghost realise that cleared the illusion and opened up satori? Say!

If you yourself come face to face with a ghost, what will you say to free it?

FREEING THE GHOST (ALTERNATIVE)

In the seventh year of the O-an era [this must be a scribal error and the date is not clear], Yorihisa went into a meditation retreat in the Emmei pavilion on Deer Mountain, outside the mountain gate of Enkakuji. His meditation was on the phrases of the Kegon Sutra:

If one would know all the Buddhas of the three worlds,

> Let him see the nature of the dharma, that all is the
> creation of mind alone,

but he had not come to know the Buddhas of the three worlds. While he was deep in meditation, it happened that the place was set on fire, but he was not aware when the roof caught alight, and perished in the flames. That night the ghost of Yorihisa appeared in front of the temple gate intoning again and again 'All the Buddhas of the three worlds, all the Buddhas of the three worlds'. The monk in charge of the temple gate reported this to the monks' hall, and Karashigawa Soryu, who held the office of tanto, went to meet the ghost. He gave a great shout 'Namu Yorihisa Butsu! (Reverence to Buddha Yorihisa!)' and the apparition vanished abruptly and never appeared again.

Tests: Where are all the Buddhas of the three worlds? Say!

What is the nature of the dharma-world like? Say!

Bring the proof of 'mind alone'.

What is this about dharma-world nature being the creation of mind alone?

The question which the monk at Kenchoji shouted with a Katzu! and the 'reverence to Buddha Yorihisa' of the Enkakuji head monk – are these ultimately the same thing or not? Explain!

Right now in front of you is the ghost of Minamoto Yoshitsune. Set him free quickly, and show the proof to the teacher.

These incidents began to be set as koans in the interviews of Dai-in, the 158th teacher at Kenchoji.

Part Four

The Ways

What are called the Ways are fractional expressions of Zen in limited fields such as the fighting arts of sword or spear, literary arts like poetry or calligraphy, and household duties like serving tea, polishing, or flower arrangement. These actions become Ways when practice is done not merely for the immediate result but also with a view to purifying, calming and focusing the psycho-physical apparatus, to attain to some degree of Zen realisation and express it.

This is not a book on the Ways, but on Zen influence in them, and little is said here about technique. It is an axiom that what applies in one Way has some application to others. Some of the examples are taken from judo, in which I can draw upon my own experience as a student and later as a teacher, and which is the most widely practised field of a Way in the West. Its disadvantage is that the technique is so complex that the effect of anything beyond technique is masked.

It is easiest to have a first experience-flash of Zen realisation in some Way like flower arrangement, in a static environment, but the combative arts are capable of a clearer expression of Zen because they require immediate response in a potentially serious situation. It is true that today they are mainly practised as sports, but the tension at time of contest is sometimes as great as at times of real danger. It is worth remembering also that Musashi, a veteran duellist, felt so nervous when brushing a picture that he could not go on (see page 174).

There is hardly any systematic instruction in the Ways as such. Most teachers teach technique and method of practice.

The stories, analogies or verses given here are to alert the student to something which, if he is seriously practising, will come occasionally in his own experience. When he has isolated it, he can cultivate it.

In this section I am presenting some of the background so that the next section of extracts from the so-called 'secret scrolls' can be appreciated. It must be said that Japanese are prone to use words very loosely; the same thing may be called spirit, essence of mind, true self, way of heaven, the great ultimate and so on. But the pairing of inspiration and formal technique (ri and ji), and heart and vital energy (shin and ki) are fairly standard in all the Ways.

The central notion of going beyond technique, and indeed beyond thought, is so unfamiliar here that it is best presented through the traditions of the knightly arts, where men risked their lives on it. The main thing to realise is, that it is not a question of established tricks simply going into action automatically as a sort of reflex. The manifestation of ri is quite different from the established techniques which have been learnt; this point should be noticed carefully – it comes again and again in the texts. It is the very reverse of mechanical repetition, because it is creative.

A Way as such is hardly ever taught directly; perhaps it cannot be taught directly – a pupil has to find out for himself. As an indication, let me say that I have known only a handful of men who could always demonstrate the Way in their judo, but quite a number who at times have had an experience of transcending the normal limits of their technique. Sometimes the man himself does not realise what has happened, and just says, 'Something sort of came to me.'

The point of having literature on the Ways is to make these happenings clear for what they are, and so encourage him to cultivate the conditions which help them to manifest. To read this kind of literature without practising a field of a Way may be annoying as well as fruitless.

Zen and the Ways

Zen masters are not keen on verbal definitions of Buddha-nature, because they are at once converted by a hearer into mental constructs like the other mental constructs which constitute his world. As such they are on an illusory basis and become obstructions to actual Buddha-realisation. However, something is said of Buddha-nature in expression:

	Buddha-without-	Monju (*wisdom*) holding a sword (*power*)
(1)	mental-constructs	(2)
	= Void	(3) Fugen (*compassion*) holding a lotus (*beauty*)

Wisdom and compassion are mental constructs of the highest clarity and serenity, through which as through a very fine veil the Void is seen and expressed. When the last veil is removed there is nothing to be said or thought, for there are no mental constructs with which to think or speak. See the story 'Painting the Nature', on p. 155. This point comes again and again in Zen.

(1) The phrase 'no mental constructs' can be bewildering or terrifying. Some people believe it would be unconsciousness, because they think that consciousness is the same as thought, which is only a movement in it. In their view, consciousness has degrees. The Soto Zen phrase 'consciously enter deep sleep and be aware of it' would be as meaningless as 'take a light into a dark room and see what the darkness looks like'. Almost nothing is known in the Western tradition about deep sleep, but the East has experimented for many centuries. Westerners might consider the many authenticated instances of inspirations in the scientific field which flashed into the mind immediately on waking. Helmholtz was a case in point.

Zen masters often use the word 'Buddha' in an absolute sense, though when they really mean business, they are more likely to use negative expressions.

(2) Is the realm of Buddhist expression, especially in poetry and art.

(3) Is the realm of everyday action. It was a special contribution of Japanese Zen to see and be able to express Buddha-nature through power and beauty in everyday things. They partially spiritualised the soldier tradition and brought inspiration into household concerns like flower-arrangement and making tea. These were called Ways.

There are many people who have no wish to transcend individuality and enter a realm beyond mental constructs, a region of transcendental aloneness. But some of them would like to experience some inspiration, to be able to enter into harmony with the universe, not simply on great occasions but at ordinary times. It is for such people that the Ways were developed. They are fragmentary manifestations of Zen which depend only minimally on circumstances; to practise them means to be able to experience a breath from beyond, to have freedom for a time at least from the drabness and cramp of life, and to become able to recognise in a particular field the cosmic life, and give it play.

The Ways have techniques, but it is not their purpose to imitate the action of cosmic life by technical means, like a pupil faithfully copying the style of his master in the absence of any inspiration of his own. The point of the techniques is to master one field thoroughly, so that the instruments of perception are able to perceive very accurately. It is then that the action of cosmic life becomes clear. Unless the eye has been trained, it is not so easy to determine what is an excellent rock garden and what is a mediocre one. Those who have not been trained in this Way or any other, will not easily be able to judge. But if an untrained man is in a badly designed garden day after day, he finds that there is a vague discomfort, a kind of physical unease, as though something needs altering but he cannot find out what it is. And in a good garden, he will find that without his particularly noticing it, there has been a calming influence on his mind; he is somehow at peace, though he does not know where the peace comes from. A trained man appreciates the garden at once, not by mental analysis, though he can do that too if it is needed. He is trained in balances and relations which cannot be specified in words.

He can appreciate what is 'speaking' through a masterpiece, and to some extent express it through his own creations.

When he begins to be able to recognise it through gardens, he may go on to recognise it elsewhere; things which he has seen every day with a jaded eye suddenly become fresh and alive. Westerners are sometimes surprised to find shops in Japan selling nothing but rocks, large and small, some of them at high prices. It can take quite a time before they can look at these rocks and really see them. Before that, there has been an internal notice 'Stones – of no value or interest.' That notice has to be dismantled before they can look.

Ri and ji

Ri and ji are well-known terms in Buddhism, meaning respectively universal truth and a particular event. In the Ways they have special meanings.

Ri is something like inspired following of the inner lines of the universal flow: it includes feeling-into the true nature of the material at hand, the space-time relations, and also the moral situation. The true inner lines of a situation are expressions of Buddha-nature, and most clearly appreciated as beauty and power. To do something 'muri' or without-ri is to force a result, using unnatural and therefore ultimately wasteful and tiring means. To shout someone down in an argument, to use advantages of wealth, prestige or physical strength to override the legitimate interests of others, to chop wood across the grain, to bang the keys of a typewriter – all these are examples of muri. It has been said that muri is doing things without love for the material and the action. To do things in conformity with ri is to feel oneness of self with them.

Ji means, in the Ways, particular techniques which have been evolved by experts; in a way these are formalizations, and ultimately imitations, of what was originally ri. They are records of ri inspirations of the past. In so far as they remain only imitations, however, they lose touch with ri; situations change constantly, and so techniques should be constantly adapting under the light of ri, or they become muri. Furthermore even a correct technique when wrongly employed may be muri.

Take the methods of writing as an example. Writing with a hard pencil is different from writing with a soft brush.

Writing from left to right, where the hand begins writing somewhere near the centre of the body and pushes out from there (note the phrase 'pen-pushing') is different from the Semitic writing from right to left where the hand is pulled in towards the central line, and different again from the Eastern system of writing in columns down the central line. But in all these systems, to press considerably more heavily than required is muri. It goes against the situation, and is an expression not of the natural lines but of something else. Again, there are those who hold a pencil near the point and have to move the hand with almost each word. This does not conform to the instrument, which has length and should be balanced on the middle finger, so that the hand moves only occasionally and the fingers need very little movement to make the pencil form the lines. An expert shorthand writer holds a pencil in this way.

Many Westerners make the final twist in wringing out a cloth by holding it across in front of them with both palms facing down. Japanese women lay the cloth pointing away, and grip it from below with the palms upward; the elbows are brought together and the hands turn against each other. This gives rather more twist. But the best way is to hold it with one palm up and the other down; the elbows go out and up as one hand comes right over and down. This sort of insight was originally ri and has become ji; probably no one thinks of it now and it is learnt purely by imitation.

Ri can show itself in any situation at all; the Ways were developed by giving special attention to a technical situation as a field for becoming aware of, and then expressing, ri by means of ji. If the inner state is to some extent clear and calm, *any* situation is an expression of ri; the point of using one special field again and again is that the manifestation of ri becomes easier to recognise. With a master of a Way, the smallest action reveals the ri fully; a prima ballerina walks more beautifully than a ballet student, and an expert could pick her out after seeing a few steps. But it is easier for the ordinary person when she is dancing.

The principle that each and every action of the Way reveals a master's ri in full is called 'ri-ji-mu-ge'; again a special meaning of a familiar Buddhist phrase. It has also the sense that ri contains the potentiality of an infinity of actions (ji).

A related principle is 'ji-ji-mu-ge', which means that each single technique of a given Way, when demonstrated by a real master, displays all the others also to an eye that can see. It is even thought that one Way can demonstrate other Ways also.

Anything can be a Way. Suppose a merchant is trying hard for financial success. That is not necessarily a Way. He may succeed, but perhaps by chance or dishonesty; again it might ruin his health. Lastly, the accumulation of wealth might absorb him completely, so that he becomes a mere watchman for the hoard, and no longer a man at all.

But he might practise his calling as a Way, as a means of spiritual development. A great fencing master of the Meiji period, famous for his perfect calm in the face of danger, was asked how he acquired it. He said, 'I got the idea from a merchant whom I knew.' Merchants in those days were supposed to be timorous folk, and this was a surprise. 'Yes,' the master continued, 'he told me about buying and selling. You buy and hope the market will go up, and if it does, you have to decide when to take the profit, or perhaps to take the profit with half and hold on with the rest. If the price goes down, you have to decide when to cut the losses. He told me that when he was young he would make a decision, and then change his mind for no reason except the nagging thought that perhaps the market would improve. And after he had sold, he would be still looking at the market figures and thinking "If only I had held on a bit more" or "If only I had got out a bit sooner!" He found he was wearing himself out with speculations and regrets. So he made a resolution to control his mind, make a decision, act on it, and afterwards never think what he might have done instead.

'I was impressed with this man's personality; he seemed to be calm and free. A big loss never disconcerted him, a big success never elated him, a big risk never daunted him. I thought him to be a master of his Way, and I applied it to my own Way.'

Another example. Miyamoto Musashi was one of the best artists in Japanese history – some of his works are now National Treasures. He was also a fearless duellist; he killed fifty-three men in duels and affrays, sometimes against great odds. Musashi was invited to brush a picture at the court of a noble. He began the picture in front of everyone, but found he was overcome with nervousness, he that had faced a group of armed attackers without any fear. He tore up the picture and said he would bring it the next day. He went home much disturbed, and then faced the paper as if it were an armed enemy, throwing himself into the state of mind in which he went into his duels. The picture was a masterpiece.

These examples show there is something of one Way in a completely different Way. A swordsman, however expert technically, who does not know ri will be like a merchant, however clever, who does not know ri. They may be successful, but they will be liable to difficulties in a crisis. The unresolved instinct of self-preservation will hamper their freedom.

One of the songs of the Way runs:

He is deluded who would learn these things merely to preserve himself.
No one can preserve his life for ever.

About a year after I had begun calligraphy, the teacher said, 'Your strokes are not too bad, but the balance of the characters is poor.' I could not make out what he meant. He would show me what he called a well-balanced character, and compare it with one of mine which he said was badly balanced; but though I could see they were different, I could not see that one was better than the other. He said suddenly, 'Look at that character as if it were a judo man. Can't you see that its balance is bad?' When I looked at it with this in mind, I did get an impression of instability, and I was able to feel that the characters he called well-balanced had a sort of poise and spring in them which I had not been able to see before. This was a big help in getting life into the characters.

In the loose Japanese way, ri and ji may be explained as 'formless' and 'with form'. A ji is a definite technique with a form, and can be seen and taught, but what is formless cannot be seen or taught. In a sense, ji can be compared with the grammatical patterns which one learns when taking up a foreign language. For a long time, one is restricted to the sentence-patterns which one knows by heart. To express a thought, one has to fit it into one of these patterns, and that means that the thought is slightly altered. In the same way, the individual techniques learnt in one of the arts will never quite fit the circumstances. Even in judo, where the techniques are very numerous, one tends to rely on certain ones which have been mastered, even if they are not absolutely appropriate. There are means of forcing the situation a little, to bring off some favourite trick. This is skilful ji, but it cannot be said to be ri. One of the first manifestations of ri is to free a man from the restriction to his special techniques.

Outsiders often think that abandoning the conscious thinking would mean that the techniques which have been learnt will go into effect as a sort of reflex, like a man changing gear without thinking about it. In fact, the very reverse happens. It is just the conscious thinking which holds the nervous energy and feeling in those habitual patterns. As a matter of fact, it is very easy to defeat a man who simply executes his techniques as a reflex. One can control his body through them. One sets off a reflex in him, and then waits with the counter.

This is one reason why an expert finds it much easier to defeat a man who has trained for a year than an absolute beginner. He knows what the partially trained man will do – he will do the technically correct things, but he will not be good enough at them. Whereas the absolute beginner has to be watched all the time, because one cannot predict his movements. Most of them are hopelessly clumsy, naturally, but occasionally there are fairly effective attacks which are theoretically unsound but which may succeed because of their very unexpectedness.

The transition from mere ji to the ri can be compared with the moment when a student of a foreign language begins to speak freely, instead of translating in his head to constructed sentences. It is quite a jump, which needs some courage, and there are students who never succeed in making it.

As a young judo man of Fourth Dan grade I had a two-part contest, as an experiment, against a kendo man of the same grade. He knew almost nothing of judo, or I of kendo. The first contest was a judo contest. Beginners generally come forward in tiny steps, teeth clenched and arms outstretched stiffly; one just picks them off at leisure.

This man gave a yell and launched himself straight at my knees like a torpedo, in a sort of flying tackle. I was so surprised that I could not get out of the way, though I managed to double up as we went down so that I finished up on top and at once tied him up, partially saving face.

When it came to the kendo contest I knew it would be useless trying to imitate kendo technique. As we came to meet each other, I slid my right hand to hold the tip of the sword-handle, and jumped in the air, holding my wrist high and swinging the bamboo sword downward in a one-handed blow to his head. A skilled kendo man protects his head by only just as much as is necessary and he made a defence to this unusual attack. But I was already much taller than most of his opponents, and the jump gave me extra height, so my bamboo sword did manage just to touch the top of his head. It would not have been a point by kendo contest standards, but it gave him a little surprise, like the one he had given me. We both agreed we had learnt something from the experiment.

Shin and ki

Shin is the technical word for 'heart', including all we call mind and more. Ki is something like 'vital spirit'. An example is better than theory: in picking up a teacup or throwing an opponent, *shin* is the notion of doing it, including the emotional colouring, *ki* is the 'feel' of initiating and continuing the movement conformably to distances and timing. What is technically called *strength* is grasping the teacup or making the throw: ki is still functioning, but with untrained people it tends to be felt less clearly when strength is being exerted.

These things may be pure and in conformity with the cosmic principle (ri), or impure and centred round an individual self.

When *shin* is *pure*, thoughts do not arise from selfishness or passion, and inspiration passes through it. When *impure*, it is distorted and dark: everything has to pass through filters of 'will this be good for me?' 'will this get me what I want?' 'how shall I look while I am doing it?' 'what shall I do if it does not come off?' 'how terrible that might be!' and so on. It is tense ('hard') and cannot adapt to changing situations.

When *ki* is *pure*, it adapts. At the time for stillness, ki fills the body and is serene. Prompted by shin at the time for action, ki is in touch with the cosmic energy – a flood of vital energy as Mencius called it. When ki is *impure* it is sluggish and uneven. At the time for stillness, there is fidgeting or vague unease; at the time for action, it wants to activate the part of the body where it is habitually concentrated (right hand or face etc.) and ignore the rest. It is slow and clumsy, not sensitive to distances and times.

When *strength* is *pure*, it conforms to the event and just so much is expended as is needed. When it is *impure*, either not enough is put forth ('weakness') or too much ('hardness').

A pure shin is serene, not plagued by worries over what happened or what may happen. It is not that there is no planning. Shin does plan, but once the known facts have been considered and the plan made, it does not worry; nor is its plan deflected by fear or hope. Shin is never absolutely pure any more than a body is ever absolutely healthy. What we call a healthy body is one which is seldom ill, and which when it becomes ill (from an accident, for example) recovers quickly. Similarly a pure shin is one which is very seldom dark or selfish, and which when it is on rare occasions clouded by such things, throws them off vigorously without much worry over them.

Shin is psychological; ki is psycho-physical; strength is physical. In the Ways, shin is the most important thing, and if it is made pure and clear, ki rights itself and the body also rights itself. 'When your heart is calm and clear, your posture and movement become correct' says one of the transmissions. If training in shin is being undertaken, training of ki and the physical training become natural, and the whole process forms a Way. If the training of shin is not being done, however, ki and the body are in service of a dark or distorted mind. They can still be trained, but the process is not natural; it is a matter of will, supported by passions like ambition. When a temporary success is attained on these lines, it distorts shin even more.

When the gaze is once fixed on the target as the bow is taken up, they must not then move from it. One's concentrated heart should be reflected in the target; what is in the hands should be forgotten as if it has been crushed to dust.

The sound of a bell in the darkness of night is a phrase illustrating the heart's attention. The essential thing is that it should be maintained at the spot below the navel, steadily. When about to begin, first take the mind firmly down there, keeping the hands light, and take up the bow without putting vigour into them. It is very bad to have any contraction of the hips and loins when taking up position; it must be done with a swelling feeling at the navel.

Drawing Up the Bow.
The eyes looking at the nose-tip form a conventional
symbol of concentration. In fact, they are fixed on the target.
(International Society for Educational Information, Tokyo)

Training of ki and the body is through technique, accepted from a teacher. This is 'tradition-received-from-another'. If shin also is trained and begins to experience inspiration, it is the 'separate tradition' of Zen.

Training of shin has been set out in the chapters on Zen in this book.

Training of ki consists in practising, deliberately and consciously, though inevitably partially, what will come of itself when shin becomes clear. The training is to prepare the instruments for the inspiration to come. It has two main aspects: training the attention and training the breathing. In many of the exercises the two are combined. Some Japanese doctors are seeking to explain the undoubted results in terms of present-day neurology. However, what has been developed by centuries of experiment in one tradition will not easily be forced into the concepts of a very different tradition; and furthermore as has been said ironically, 'If it agrees with the neurology of today, it will certainly not agree with the neurology of thirty years hence.'

Here is one set of exercises out of many.

(1) Sit in a firm posture; it is worth mastering one of the meditation postures, in spite of the difficulties at the beginning. An easy one is to sit on the ground with the hips on a cushion, and the left foot on the right thigh.

Tie a cloth sash just under the navel, and put a pebble inside the sash so that it presses slightly at the tanden (elixir-field) point, one to two inches below the navel. Another way is to make a big knot in the sash and set it at this point.

Breathe in slowly, taking four or five seconds, and feel that the current of breath is going down to that point and as it were swelling it out like a little balloon, so that it presses against the pebble. When the in-breath is complete, hold it and pull in the muscles of the lower abdomen slightly. Feel you are pulling in and up a little with the muscles, and that this in-and-up pressure is meeting the out-and-down pressure of the breath at the tanden point. Of course inhaled air does not actually get down to the navel, but the easiest way to come to feel the current is to feel that it does. It is an experimental process.

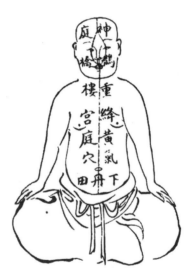

Tanden at navel. The diagram pictures the centres and currents of vital energy along the front of the body. Reading from the bottom they are: the Field of the Elixir (tanden), the Cave of Life, the Yellow Court, the Red Palace, the Pagoda, the Magpie Bridge and the Divine Court. In Zen and the Ways, the important preliminary point of concentration is the tanden.

When this is being practised, you may feel a little growl in the throat, much as someone who is lifting a heavy weight with the abdominal muscles. Some teachers make the Katzu! shout with an abrupt tension at the tanden.

Hold the pressure for five seconds.

Breathe out in about five seconds, and relax the abdominal pressure but try to retain the sensation at the tanden.

This exercise should be repeated ten minutes morning and evening. If you feel out of breath, stop the practice and take a few breaths in any way you like. Then begin again.

One of the secret transmission scrolls of a Jujutsu school, dated about 1710, comments on an exercise of this type:

Keeping in a formal posture, exhale and inhale, thinking that the breath is passing to just below the navel. This is in fact the natural course of feeling the breath, but because people move badly their inner organs are compressed, and the vital current is felt only as in the chest. So people soon get out of breath when they are hurrying, and when they speak their voice has no carrying power and is not clear. The defect is bad breathing. So we must train to make the breathing correct.

And it is said in a tradition of our school: breath is the pulse of the mind. When the mind is agitated, the breath is always irregular. The instruction is to practise improving the breathing, and that will help to calm the mind.

Most people take up this kind of exercise enthusiastically for two or three weeks, and then drop it. It needs to be done for two or three months at least before it shows itself, though in some cases results come sooner.

There are many hints about it in the traditions. Musashi in his classic of the sword called 'Five Rings' remarks on the stance before a duel, 'Tense the abdomen so that your hips do not bend. What is called "the wedge" means to push your short sword into your belt so that it comes tight against the abdomen.' The knot of the belt was just below the navel, and Musashi's advice is to help the fencer to concentrate attention there. He adds that this should also be practised in daily life.

For some time, holding attention at the tanden during ordinary activities is an artificial affair. Those who are not doing any real training but trying it only out of curiosity, find they become irritated and abandon it. But when it has been seriously practised for a time, physical movement changes; it becomes easier to use the body as a unity.

(2) Practice tanden meditation first in simple operations, for example polishing the top of a table. This has a technique, though a simple one, and it should be learnt. The practise is to hold attention at the central tanden point instead of letting it be fixed in the polishing hand. After some weeks' practice, there is an experience of balance, and the body suddenly feels 'alive'. The long strokes are made from the loins – a slight movement at the centre moves the hand at the circumference.

This is sometimes a marked change, and when the practiser first becomes aware of it he usually becomes excited and 'interested'. His concentration is dispersed. The disturbance sometimes remains for weeks, upsetting him every time he tries to practise. It is well to be familiar with this situation; it arises in a heart still full of self-reference. This is why the teachers say that a special training of ki alone, however intensive, without training the heart, is ultimately self-defeating.

(3) After some months, or perhaps longer, attention is expanded to the whole body. The vital current is taken in with the breath and felt to fill the whole body from the tips of toes and fingers to the top of the head. While breath is held, the body is felt to be full of light, and empty and cool as breath is expelled. In daily life, awareness of the entire body is cultivated. When writing, every few minutes the writer stops and flexes his left hand, presses his feet on the floor and so on, trying to become vividly aware of the whole body. If he can, he stretches. Later he can keep total awareness without having to recall it so often.

In the West, individuals discover these things occasionally. Nietzsche used to say, 'When I write, I write with my whole body.' Pianists have a tradition that parts of the Hammerklavier Sonata should be played with the hips. But there is no general tradition to co-ordinate these glimpses.

(4) A more advanced exercise in ki training is designed to facilitate inspiration. For a long time, a pupil cannot shake off his attachments when performing an action; he hopes for or dreads what it may bring, or considers how he is doing. Perhaps he may try to shake off such thoughts by alcohol or another drug, but then he drops into another and lower mental phase, inertia or silliness. When a student

of the Ways first tries to allow the cosmic current to flow through him, either he simply stops moving, or else he tries to imitate what he thinks it ought to be like, and his movements become nervously busy and over-reactive. Either way, nothing significant happens.

The first phase of this exercise is to use the breath. For his polishing he selects a wide surface, and makes long strokes with the cloth feeling the tanden as usual. Now he begins to breathe in to say five strokes and out to the same number (no holding of the breath at the beginning). After a time, he forgets the tanden and feels that the breath current is brimming over from his arm and doing the action itself. At first he will just feel self-conscious, but later he feels that it is so. His muscles relax a good deal, and the movements become smooth, regular and easy. He does not have the sensation of putting out effort; the breath itself seems to be moving hand and cloth.

In this exercise, when the movement is so to say 'handed over' to the breath, it tends to go slower for a little, and then picks up speed. Most students lose their calm when the movement slows, and put out a little voluntary effort to rectify it. This breaks up the exercise.

(5) The final stage is to abandon breath also. When shin becomes clear, the cosmic life acts directly through it and through ki. Take a case where it should be easiest for this to happen, where what is required is simply relaxation.

In archery, release of the arrow is a central problem. The aim has been taken, and it is just a question of relaxing the tension of the right hand, without making any other movement. But the decision, 'Now I will do it' affects posture and aim. So it must be a decision that is no decision, and that is no easy thing. One of the Songs of the Ways is:

To think of not-thinking is to think another thought:
Giving up thinking and not-thinking, rest in natural purity.

One of the secret archery transmissions says, 'The action of releasing the arrow is to be not an action of the individual but an action of the universe. Then the arrow will not be deflected even a fraction from the aim, since I am myself unconscious of its release.'

Another says, 'Release of the arrow is without thought, without idea, like a dew-drop falling from a leaf, or a fruit falling when the time is ripe.'

But for a long time students cannot attain this. They wait for the universe to make its move, they wait for the fruit to fall. And nothing happens. Finally in impatience they irritably jerk their hand open and the arrow goes wide. (It is interesting to know that Western archers were aware of the problem – a saying is attributed to Robin Hood to the effect that it is doubtful whether any arrow has ever been perfectly released.)

In Japan, the students are therefore told first to put their attention on ki, as a stepping-stone to being open to the cosmic current. The technique of ki has various forms, but one of them is to take it that the in-breath as it passes through the nostrils makes the sound A, and the out-breath a long UM. (Some schools make them the other way round, but that is not important here.) The bow is drawn to a long in-breath, to the A; then with the out-breath, the arrow shoots off to the sound of a long UM. It is much easier to abandon the arrow to the breath as it were, without a conscious decision 'Now'. But still, it needs a good deal of practice. And again, after a success excitement often breaks up the mental poise.

A passage from the transmission of the Yoshida school of archery (late sixteenth century) runs:

Release of the arrow is to be as if the string snapped. The bow does not know; I also do not know – this is the important thing. Beginners however have to try to attain this state by pulling the bow and taking aim with the A breath, and releasing with the UM sound of the breath.

With beginners, breathing tends to go fast or to be held, or to come and go in gasps and jerks, and all this has to be overcome by training. The same thing applies to all arts; unless this one thing is mastered, the art is not mastered. Though a man may shoot successfully, if his breath is uneven he cannot be called a master.

The text explains later that however great the technical skill, it is liable to fail in a crisis unless the breath has been mastered.

There are many other points concerned with shin and ki, but it is no advantage to have them explained. They have to be discovered for oneself. One who practises with reverence can find the Way in the most boring and repetitive jobs of life; one day his heart will become clear and calm, there is inner brightness and emptiness, the sensations and movements stand out with brilliant clarity but without interior reactions. This may not happen often, but even to seek it is to find a new meaning in life.

Isshin and zanshin

Isshin (one-heart) means to throw oneself wholly into the action without any other thought at all. Zanshin (remaining-heart) means some awareness still remaining. Some of the texts give both, some of them do not mention zanshin at all, and some of them mention it but say that the heading 'zanshin' means that there must be *no* zanshin.

With a spear, isshin is to commit one's body wholly to the thrust; in a judo throw, it means to throw one's body and heart at the opponent. If the action is technically defective, or the opponent more skilful, it will miss; then one is generally in an unfavourable position. On the other hand, the mere impetuosity and immediacy and completeness of the movement may have so upset him that he cannot utilise his momentary advantage.

Still, in theory might it not be better to take into account possible failure, and keep something back in order to be able to adapt to it? But then, the 'one-heart' will be broken into two: one saying 'everything into the throw' and the other 'what if it fails?' The latter is called a fox-doubt, and it infects the physical movement, to cause hesitation.

Similarly, if the attack is successful, must a new isshin be formed to deal with a new opponent?

The schools which speak of zanshin take it as an awareness which is wide and unmoving, and which contains the isshin. The immediate awareness is thrown into the action, and yet something remains, unconscious? conscious?, which can handle a failure or even a success. This is zanshin. It must not be consciously aimed at, as that would split the 'one-heart'.

In a sense the one-heart is the ji or particular technique, and the remaining-heart is the ri or universal principle which manifests in particular situations but is not exhausted in them.

Isshin is the unity of the wave, zanshin is unity of the water. Isshin defeats an opponent at a time and place, by a technique. Zanshin is awareness of the whole process of defeating opponents, and wider than that, defeating them with minimum harm to them, and wider than that, for a good purpose, and wider than that...

In the verses, zanshin is referred to as 'water holding the moon'.

Not setting the mind

> The mind turns in accordance with the ten
> thousand things;
> The pivot on which it turns is verily hard to know.
> *Zen verse (much quoted in the Ways)*

Like many of the Buddhist verses and aphorisms, this verse about not letting the mind get set, but keeping it freely turning on a pivot, seems vaguely 'wise', but is soon abandoned in practice. A fencer comes out without setting his mind on his opponent's techniques or his own, and his movement becomes slack, so that he gets a hit on the head at once. The calligrapher goes to write without letting his mind be set on the proper way of writing the character; the result is a sprawling mess. It is true that in this last case, he may persuade himself that he has written well, in an unorthodox manner; but the archer who has missed by a mile has no such refuge. One of the advantages of the martial ways is that the result is so immediately apparent. In any case, after a few failures the whole attempt is abandoned.

As the classic says, 'those who are not training in a tradition will find it hard to understand.' The teacher has to supply one or two concrete examples from the particular tradition. Here is one from the judo tradition. In Tokugawa times, one of the big Jujutsu schools lost three of its best men, killed at night in the street. In each case there was only one mark on the body, a stab in the abdomen, slightly to the right side. It was guessed that these killings were done by a member of a rival school, with which there was a feud on, but the puzzle was how these three highly skilled men could have been killed by one clean stab. If they had been overcome by numbers there would have been other marks; a single man, even though armed, could hardly have finished the fight with one blow, especially a thrust to the abdomen which is easily checked.

The experts finally worked out how it had been done. There are only two effective ways of using the stabbing knife, (1) from below to the abdomen, and (2) down from above on to the neck and shoulder. Skilled Jujutsu men were well practised in the defences to both of these attacks. An expert could tell which attack was coming by observing the position of the attacker's right hand: if the thumb is in front, the attack will come down, and if it is to the rear, the attack is upward. Before the blade is actually visible, the defender's body is already moving into the defensive reaction.

The other Jujutsu school had discovered how to make use of this fact. Their man was holding the knife reversed; his left hand holding the hilt, and the right hand holding only the sheath. This right hand had the thumb prominently displayed – in front. So the defender was moving to intercept a downward blow, but when that came it was being made with the sheath, while the blade moved upwards unopposed.

This is an example of getting the mind set on one thing, namely the position of the opponent's thumb, which in the ordinary way is the key to the situation. Does this mean then that the thumb is not to be noticed? No. It is to be noticed, but not at the expense of the whole situation. As a matter of fact, the opponent's posture is not the normal one of a man about to draw a knife with his right hand. The opponent is holding the knife in fact in his left hand, and he will have to advance his left foot to use it. If we look at the posture in the third set of pictures, we see that from the very beginning the knife-man has his left foot level with his right foot, whereas in the normal case it is well back. An experienced judo expert, who does not let his mind become *set* on the thumb position, will find something 'unusual' in the situation, and will correspondingly keep a freedom of action. He will not be tied to a mechanical defence reaction.

Followers of any Way should consider how technical excellence in a particular point gradually becomes mechanical, and creativity is lost. Technique, like logic, can only operate by ignoring certain aspects of a situation as insignificant; it works well in nine cases out of ten, but in the tenth case the disregarded aspects are in fact decisive. In the tenth case, absolute reliance on technique, or logic, can be disastrous. The mind becomes set on them, and cannot adapt. Technique is to be utilised, but it must not become the master, as it does when it is worshipped by a mind set on it.

Thrust without thrusting

Do not thrust with the mind,
Do not thrust with the hands,
Let the spear make the thrust –
   Thrust without thrusting.
   From the Hundred Verses of the Spear

This verse has a relation to the interviews described in koan no. 44 of the Shonankattoroku, where the Zen teacher says, 'No spear in the hands, no hands on the spear. If you don't understand, your art of the spear is a little affair of the hands alone.' The interview with Gio (arrived in Japan 1246) is probably the first reference to Zen in the Ways in Japanese literature (p. 147).

There is a tendency to read a contradiction like 'thrust without thrusting' as a poetic conceit. Perhaps it means that the thrust should be in a calm spirit, without passionate desire to hit the opponent? The normal thrust after all includes, in fact is based on, this desire, so perhaps a thrust made without it would be a thrust-without-thrusting? Others with a smattering of Buddhism say that it means to make the thrust without 'identifying' oneself with it.

But what does this amount to? Suppose the practice spear is passed across, with the direction 'now thrust without the usual passionate desire to score a hit, as you have said'. The spear moves in a vague way, the opponent at once counters. Or again one may be asked to make the thrust 'without identifying' with it; here again the spear makes no definite movement and is at once brushed aside in a counter.

A great advantage of the knightly arts, considered as Ways, is that the result is so directly apparent. A dabbler in art can brush a few tentative strokes in a spirit of 'non-identification' as he thinks, and if they are not appreciated as inspired, he may still think that his inspiration is not recognised. But in a spear contest a vigorous blow in the chest from an opponent's spear is a sufficient answer.

'Thrust without thrusting.' It is a riddle which has to be solved in practice. A Westerner is not likely to have enough faith in the teacher or the tradition to be able to tackle it as it stands. He often has a fairly complete faith in the power of intellect to grasp realities, and the anti-intellectual formulation – thrust without thrusting – produces recurring doubts. He may feel that it is unscientific.

Some Westerners need to investigate whether such things do occur here, and whether indeed they are at the very base of our scientific tradition. Take a parallel phrase from Zen: 'Think without thinking.' What can it mean? It is essential not to shunt the problem off on to a mental siding. Take it in concrete terms: suppose a problem in physics. In what sense could it be solved by 'thinking without thinking'?

The Nobel prize-winner Enrico Fermi, who led the construction of the first self-sustaining nuclear reactor, made many original contributions to various phases of physics. He had a very pure reverence for truth – his colleagues reported that when in a discussion it became clear to everyone that Fermi was right, he would at once change the subject. He never took pleasure in the fact that *he* was right. In Zen, this kind of personal generosity in discussion is said to be a mark of purity of heart.

Fermi was asked by an Indian physicist, Chandrasekhar, about the process of discovery in physics, and he replied,

> I will tell you how I came to make the discovery which I suppose is the most important one I have made. We were working very hard on the neutron induced radioactivity and the results we were obtaining made no sense. One day, as I came to the laboratory, it occurred to me that I should examine the effect of placing a piece of lead before the incident neutrons. And instead of my usual custom, I took great pains to have the piece of lead precisely machined. I was clearly dissatisfied with something: I tried every 'excuse' to postpone putting the piece of lead in its place. When finally, with some reluctance, I was going to put it in its place, I said to myself, 'No: I do not want this piece of lead here; what I want is a piece of paraffin.' It was just like that: with no advance warning, no conscious prior reasoning. I immediately took some odd piece of paraffin I could put my hands on and placed it where the piece of lead was to have been.

This kind of thing is what a Zen man would call 'thinking without thinking'. It was not some unconscious process of inference; there was no way in which an inference could have been reached – given the knowledge of the time – about the effects of slowing the neutron beam through paraffin.

A Zen teacher would also note that when Fermi was told, at the early age of fifty-three, that he was going to die of cancer in six months, he met the announcement with detachment and calm. He remarked to his Indian colleague,

'The loss is not as great as one might think. Now you tell me, will I be an elephant next time?' The joke dispelled the gloom of his friends, and this kind of carefree attitude in the face of whatever may happen is often referred to in the secret traditions of the martial arts, and of other Ways also. It is held to be an essential element in helping inner inspiration to manifest.

Such flashes of inspiration are at the root of progress in science, yet they have no place in our official accounts. Fermi had been thinking very hard about the problem; as he says, 'the results made no sense'. When the moment came, he did not actually think of the paraffin; there was no sequence of the kind which we define as 'thinking'. But nor can we say that he did not think of it. It is thinking without thinking, and the concept may not be so foreign to us as we may have supposed. It is only that we do not have a name for it, and cannot fit it into our world view.

This kind of dramatic case is useful to loosen the hold of materialistic preconceptions, fostered by the immense prestige of science (though the Newtons and Einsteins are not materialists). The first thing is to acknowledge that there can be such a thing as inspiration. Fermi's inspiration was not a guess, as is clearly shown by his account, and it was cognitive, it brought accurate information. An Eastern scientist may be a thorough-going materialist in his practice, but he tends not to be so dogmatic about it as in the West. He knows there are such cases, and has an open mind about them. Whereas many Western scientists – according to a prominent Japanese one – have closed minds: 'they say they are open to consider any evidence on any question, but in fact on some questions they have already made up their minds, with or without evidence.'

In the end, these things are only finally convincing when they happen to oneself. Stories about them and evidences for them have value only in giving a man confidence to try to experience inspiration himself.

One of the contributions which Japanese tradition may make to world culture is to show that inspiration may manifest in any situation, however trivial it may seem. In the West, inspiration is usually thought of as applying to great situations, and then in an intellectual or aesthetic context. The Ways as developed in Japan have also been concerned with the aesthetic, but even more with spiritualization of the concerns of life, whether the profession of the warrior or a household activity like serving tea. The notion was not unknown in the Indian and Chinese traditions, but it was not systematically applied to ordinary things. However, take this example from the classic of Chuang-tzu. (This is the old translation by James Legge.)

His cook was cutting up an ox for the ruler Wanhui. Whenever he applied his hand, leaned forward with his shoulder, planted his foot, employed the pressure of his knee, in the audible ripping off of the skin and slicing operation of the knife, the sounds were all in regular cadence. Movements and sounds proceeded as in the dance of the 'Mulberry Forest' and the notes of Ching Shau. The ruler said, 'Ah, admirable! That your art should have become so perfect!' The cook laid down his knife and replied, 'What your servant loves is the method of the Way [tao – in Japanese, do], something in advance of any art. When I first began to cut up an ox, I saw nothing but the [entire] carcase. After three years I ceased to see it as a whole. Now I deal with it in a spirit-like manner, and do not look at it with my eyes. The use of my senses is discarded, and my spirit acts as it wills.

Observing the natural lines [my knife) slips through the great crevices and slides through the great cavities, taking advantage of the facilities thus presented. My art avoids the membraneous ligatures, and much more the great bones.

A good cook changes his knife every year [it gets blunt] from the cutting; an ordinary cook changes his every month – it gets broken. Now my knife has been in use for nineteen years; it has cut up several thousand oxen, and yet its edge is as sharp as if it had newly come from the whetstone. There are the interstices of the joints, and the edge of the knife has no thickness; when that which is so thin enters where the gap is, how easily it moves along! The blade has more than room enough. Still, whenever I come to a complicated joint, and see that there will be some difficulty, I proceed cautiously and carefully, not allowing my eyes to wander from the place, and moving my hand slowly. Then by a very slight movement of the knife, the part is quickly separated and drops like a clod of earth to the ground. Then standing up with the knife in my hand I look all round, and in a leisurely manner and serenely I wipe it clean and put it in its sheath.'

The ruler Wanhui said, 'Excellent! I have heard the

words of my cook, and learned from them how to cultivate inner vitality.'

This passage shows important elements in the Ways, but application to ordinary affairs of daily life was not systematically cultivated in the Chinese traditions. There are more of these stories in Taoist classics, but they are only fragmentary hints. The operations of the cook are beautifully described – 'like a dance, movements and sounds in rhythm', showing that the whole body took part as a unity. As a rule in such operations the lower part of the body remains fixed, with arms and shoulders alone active. To overcome this great defect is essential in cultivation of the Ways.

We may also notice that though the cook says, 'I do not look at it with my eyes', he later remarks that when there is a difficult place, he does not allow his eyes to wander away. And though he says 'my spirit acts as it wills', he also says that in those difficult places he proceeds cautiously. The inspiration is not like automatic writing, or a sneeze, where something happens that does not involve the whole of the man.

When these things are actually tried, when a man picks up a brush to try painting from inspiration, or when a judo or kendo man tries simply not thinking about technique or winning or losing, what happens? The short answer is, nothing happens. He holds the brush for a little, waiting for something to occur. Then in an embarrassed way he makes a few tentative strokes, or else he tenses his whole body and tries to jerk off a masterpiece in a fever of excitement. In neither case is the result of any significance. In the case of the judo man, he usually finds himself flat on his back in a matter of seconds, even if he has taken the precaution to select a considerably inferior opponent.

After a few such experiences, most people give up any attempt to attain inspiration. Some cease to believe in it, while others push it into a mental limbo, true perhaps on some high level but not as a practical fact.

But a student who still retains his keenness is told to practise hard, and to meditate on, and realise, the 'moon on the water'. Here are a few traditional verses about it:

> The water does not think of giving it lodging
> Nor the moon of lodging there –
>> How clear the reflection!

> The moon's reflection is deep in the lake,
> Yet you can carry it away in a dipper
>> If your hand is steady.

> Over Sarusawa Lake when the mist is thick;
> The rising and setting of the moon
>> No man knows.

> The water does not think of giving it lodging,
> Nor the moon of lodging there –
>> How calm the water of Lake Hirosawa!

A single sentence which comes in several traditions is: 'When you are waiting, it is Moon in the Water.'

*About to dash the brush onto the paper to write the character for 'dragon.'
The connection between brush and sword is clearly shown.
(From the dojo of Omori Sogen Roshi)*

Falling

A drunken man falls from his carriage without hurting himself seriously, remarked Chuang-tsu over two thousand years ago. This is because his body is relaxed and his spirit 'entire'. But actually confronting a fall, this knowledge is no use; the body automatically contracts and stiffens.

A judo student has to be trained to fall, to meet the ground all together instead of trying to keep off the ground and taking all the shock on one small point such as the wrist. After a time he can meet a fall on the judo mat, and if the teacher says 'Fall' he can do so.

Still something is lacking. One day the teacher comes up behind him quietly, and pulls him sharply over. If he falls then properly, it is 'part of him', he does it without knowing what he is doing. If the surprise makes him stiffen up, his training is incomplete.

Even after he can pass this test, there is one more. One day he will fall over, on ice or whatever it is, wholly by chance, and will fall properly. Once this has happened, it affects his walking and his judo practice, because before he had always been subconsciously afraid of falling. Now the ground is his friend.

The application in the Ways is to falls in life. To be able to take a disaster or a great failure, with the whole personality, without shrinking back from it, like the big smack with which the judo man hits the ground. Then to rise at once.

Not to be appalled at a moral fall. Yet it is not that it does not matter. The judo man tries by every means not to be thrown, but when he is thrown it does not hurt him and

ZEN AND THE WAYS

in a sense it does not matter. It matters immensely, and yet it does not matter.

'Falling seven times, and getting up eight.'

Faith

If you feel that the teacher is a real teacher
Then give up your own ideas, and learn.
First verse of the Hundred Verses of the Spear

If a pupil comes to him simply to get a little skill in the art, the teacher finds his strong point, what comes most naturally to him as he now is, and develops that. It gives quick results and fulfils the end.

But if someone comes who wants to master the art and give himself to it, the instruction is often the reverse. The teacher has to find out the weak points, and by special training bring them up to the level of the rest. Then he develops the whole range together.

This kind of training produces in the pupil at various times a crisis of faith: faith in the teacher, and faith in himself. The teacher has to modify his instruction according to the fluctuating levels of faith.

Suppose there is a bad weakness, due perhaps to some inherited inaptitude. The quickest way of all is to concentrate on that. A pupil of great faith and cheerfulness is prepared to look a fool for two or three months, failing and failing and failing again at what he cannot do, and not permitted to show what he *can* do. Not many are prepared to go through this; and even those who have been through it may not be willing to face it again, once they have got a little status and reputation.

So the teacher sometimes has to modify the programme. He sets them certain exercises to develop the weak points, but also gives some scope for displaying the strong points. This training is not nearly so quick, and it has something unsatisfactory about it. Normally, an ordinary pupil's strong points are distorted, because he uses them not merely as they should be used, but also to cover up the weak points. From the expert point of view, what the pupil thinks are strong points are not really so strong.

This can be seen in many small things in life. Take a job of packing a number of small things of varied shapes into a box. The trained expert stands directly in front of the box and uses the hands alternately. As one hand is fitting a piece in, the other hand is reaching out for another one. But a man who is strongly right-handed stands rather to the left of the box, and hardly uses the left hand at all. The body posture is distorted, and the right hand has to do much more reaching out than should be necessary. The right hand is moving fast and skilfully, but compared with an expert using both hands, the whole process is strained, tiring and slow. Yet many people if they are asked to develop the use of the left hand in this situation become uneasy and say, 'I can't do it.' They have not got faith in the instructor or in themselves. They are unable to hold on to the conviction that in the end the performance will be more accurate, faster, and less tiring. All they know is that it produces a drop in effectiveness now, and they go back to one-handedness with a sense of relief. It feels more natural.

Students of the Ways must see clearly that in an untrained man the intellect is like a barrister. It argues clearly and logically, but the aim is not truth, but to reach a predetermined conclusion. The barrister is paid by one party, and he tries to find evidence and reasoning to further the interests of that party. The two barristers argue as though they were concerned to establish truth, without fear or favour, but in fact each of them is driving towards a particular conclusion. If they exchanged briefs, they would be using each other's arguments. In the same way, in an untrained personality, the intellect is briefed by the particular emotion which is in the ascendant at the moment. Fear says, 'I find this unfamiliar and alarming; find me reasons for not going on.' Boredom will say, 'I want a change; find me reasons why it would be better to have a break from my practice.' Pride says, 'I cannot stand this continual failure; find me reasons for going back to my usual ways where at any rate I had some success.' Doubt says, 'After all, does the teacher understand me? Is this my path? Probably he mechanically gives this kind of instruction to everyone, and does not realise that I am an exception.'

At these times what Buddhists call Bright Wisdom must intervene and say, 'No. This is a qualified teacher and we selected him and resolved to train under him. He tells us that these unfamiliar practices are the quickest way. He tells us we shall be able to do them. What motive would he have for deceiving us?' Bright Wisdom represents the whole of the personality, and is supported by the whole and not paid by just one individual mood; it is like the judge, paid by the whole community, who protects the community from those who for a moment are in a position of power.

Often the pupil's faith in himself depends on his faith in the teacher. But later on there may be a conflict. It is a curious fact that with a certain type of pupil, the first manifestation of faith in himself is when the teacher tells him,

'Now *that* you will never master completely – don't make that a main objective. You must know about it, and do a bit of it, but in the main you should rely on this and this and this' and he explains why. Quite often this kind of pupil thinks, 'Why shouldn't I become expert at it?' As a personal example, I spent three years trying to master a throw called Hanegoshi, which I saw marvellously performed by a famous judo expert T. Kotani, when he visited London with Dr Kano in 1935. My own teacher told me, 'You will never be able to use that as a contest technique; you had better stick to Haraigoshi which is similar but suits your build better. Your physique and movement is quite different from Mr Kotani's.' But I was captivated by what I had seen, and in addition to the full training programme which my teacher set, I also practised about twenty minutes a day at the Hanegoshi. The teacher said no more, but after three years I had to admit he was right. I could only bring it off against much weaker opponents whom I could throw easily in any other way. The teacher remarked, 'That was a good experience for you. Remember it when you come to teach. I did not say any more because the Hanegoshi is similar in many ways to Haraigoshi, and I knew the practice you put in at it would help you with your own throw in the end.'

He referred to this incident once again much later on, and said, 'At least you didn't complain that I had told you wrong. You tried for yourself, and you found out. And you did keep up your practice with the things which I had told you to do. Some of them here try a throw for three weeks and then come to me and say, "I've been trying it for three weeks now and still can't do it. Are you sure it is going to suit me?" I feel like saying to them, "I myself have been trying it for thirty years and I can't do it properly either!" I don't say it, but it has taken me a long time to get used to all these little doubts which Western people seem to have all the time.'

Later when I came to teach I realised the truth of his words. Sometimes after watching a beginner for some time carefully, I have concluded that his progress can be along such and such a path. I can see clearly in my mind's eye how his one-sidedness can change to a co-ordination of the whole body; how his nervous timidity can develop into very quick reactions; how his shortness of arm can be turned to advantage by holding the tips of the opponent's sleeves. In my experience I have seen each of these transformations several times, and been through similar ones myself. I estimate that he has enough interest in judo to keep up the practice.

But when I have told him what to do, after about three months I see a doubt coming up in his mind because he doesn't see much success and he seems to be getting worse. There is nothing more to tell him when he asks me about it. The seeds are there, and it is a question of watering them by practice, and waiting. When one is inexperienced as a teacher, one gets quite worried about the pupil's situation; his anxieties rub off on to the teacher as it were. But an older teacher realises it is useless to worry or even think about it. The thinking has been done already, and a proper programme has been carefully worked out to suit this pupil. Either he will follow it out, or he will not.

Dragon masks

With age, a judo expert's speed begins to decline, and he has to find means to offset this against up-and-coming opponents. One of them is to establish a psychological ascendency over a younger man who may be actually stronger in fighting ability.

This can be done by preventing the junior from estimating the respective standards of ability. An experienced man can make an estimate easily in most cases by merely looking at the movement, but a young man generally cannot do it without something definite to work on, and he can be prevented from getting the information.

The senior's *attacking* policy is to attempt to throw only when it is certain to succeed – in other words, never to fail in a throw. This often means waiting for quite a time till the opponent takes some risk and so gives an opportunity. But promising young judo men take risks all the time; they get bored unless they are trying something. The senior's *defending* policy is never to take any risk himself, so that the opponent never scores. This is not difficult for a patient man.

The physical result of these policies is that in a practice of say six minutes the junior makes dozens of attempts but does not score at all, whereas the senior makes perhaps three attempts and each time with success. The psychological result is that the senior appears invincible. Every time he attempted a throw, he succeeded. Reason may urge that after all he did not try more than three throws in six minutes. But perhaps he did not want to. Who is to say? The lower grade feels helpless.

A seasoned judo expert has experienced this situation from both sides, and knows that in spite of attempts to reason away the conviction of helplessness, it remains very powerful. He sometimes wonders how he could have been taken in by it for so long as a young man, and he wonders why the young men whom he impresses today do not simply see through it.

The paralysing awe of the senior can go on for a good time till one day the senior tries a throw and fails. Immediately the situation changes; the junior realises that under certain circumstances he can successfully resist the attack. He now has a measure – out of four attacks in the practice, he has resisted one. The magic spell is broken, and the higher grade appears as a mortal with weaknesses of his own. Once there is a measure, the young man's ambition comes up with confidence – 'now I can only stop one in four, but I will fight to make it one in three, and then finally I'll be able to stop them all'.

The essence of the matter is that previously he did not know how wide was the gap between them, and so he could have no ambition of closing it, but now he has a way of measuring it and confidence that it can be reduced and then annihilated.

The same principle applies in struggles against interior enemies. If someone is irrationally afraid of aeroplanes, or electric machines, or figures, or getting up in the morning, he tends to regard these things as unconquerable. In such a case it is essential to make a space in life and establish one clear success. A student can put aside one week during which he is prepared to change his life. During that week he may support his resolution by reading up statistics, if his intellect is one that puts up this sort of argument; he can find out, for instance, that it is safer to travel by plane than by car. If it is a question of getting up in the morning, the resistance is more likely to take the form of a headache or stomach-ache. Then the important thing is to go on into the day with the headache or any other ache; it is only for a week, but it does have to be for that week.

After a week of getting up early, or practising rapid adding, or planning and executing an air trip to another part of the country, or getting someone to give a lesson on an electric circuit, the awe-inspiring magical threat of these things disappears. It may not be necessary to go further with them. The point is, that if it is necessary, now or later, he is able to do it by a reasonable effort. He is not shrinking back before he has even tried.

In Zen this is called by various names, and one of them is 'hitting through the dragon mask'. Students of Zen are made to practise a good deal of austerity, and one purpose is to get them used to hitting the dragon masks and finding out that they are only cardboard after all. Experiences of this kind in small things gives confidence when it comes to hitting the final dragon mask.

Part Five
Texts of the Ways

The secret scrolls of the various Ways, generally given only to graduating pupils, were mainly memoranda of instruction given verbally. They were made deliberately obscure so that outsiders who might see them would not be able to understand.

They are mostly in brief paragraphs with a heading, or else in verse. Sometimes there is only the heading, with under it the words 'oral tradition' (kuden).

There is a good deal of repetition – some of the verses, for instance, are identical in scrolls of sword, spear and archery.

The extracts given here have not to my knowledge been translated before. I have tried to choose representative sections which are yet not so obscure as to defy translation. Readers who are themselves engaged in some activity as a Way will be able to find an application in them.

I have chosen from the traditions of the martial schools because these involve the problem of response, which Ways like tea or calligraphy do not, at least in an overt form. And there is the further point that, by historical accident, the Ways developed in Japan mainly through warriors. There are movements in the Tea Ceremony, for instance, which derive from those made by fencers and archers.

The first set of extracts, from the Heihokadensho classic, show the influence of the Zen priest Takuan, who himself wrote two works on parallel lines but from the Buddhist standpoint only.

Heihokadensho
(about AD 1630)

It was said of old: 'The fighting man is an ill-omened instrument; the Way of Heaven has no love for him, yet has to make use of him, and this is the Way of Heaven.' The bow and arrow, the swords short and long, are unblessed tools of fighting and of ill omen. Therefore as the Heavenly Way is a way of giving life to things, and these are the contrary, being means of killing, they are really instruments of ill omen. They can be said to take part in transgression of the Way of Heaven. And yet, when it is unavoidable, making use of them to kill people is also said to be the Way of Heaven. How can this be?

Formal exercises with the sword. The wide stance with toes pointing in almost opposite directions was characteristic of one school. It enables the swordsman to switch the direction of his defence and counter-attack very rapidly.

Two universal postures with the sword.

An unusual parry. Note that the left foot is forward as against the orthodox right stance of the attacker.

With the breeze of spring, flowers bloom and their colours vie with each other: with the frost of autumn, leaves fall and the trees are desolate. This is fulfilment and falling away in the Way of Heaven. When a thing is completely fulfilled, Heaven strikes it. Man too, on the tide of fortune, takes to evil; when that evil becomes full, Heaven strikes it. This is when Heaven uses fighting for its ends. Ten thousand people are oppressed by the wickedness of one man, and by killing that one man the other ten thousand are given new life. So there the sword which kills is indeed a blade which gives life. There is righteousness in using the arts of fighting in this way. Without righteousness, it is merely a question of killing other people and avoiding being killed by them. Consider carefully what the arts of fighting, Heiho, really are. [Translator's note: Heiho includes strategy and tactics.]

There is a Heiho which is simply oneself confronting someone else, using two swords. One wins and the other loses, and this is petty Heiho – the winning or losing is of no real importance. The great Heiho is when in the victory of one man, Heaven is victorious, and in the defeat of the other, Heaven yields.

LEAVING THE TRAINING METHODS, YET NOT GOING AGAINST THEM

When he has completed the training and has accumulated a great fund of practice experience, he moves hands and feet and body without the mind being involved; this is leaving the training methods without going against them, and now there is freedom in using any technique (waza) at all. As to the mind at that time, the devil himself cannot guess its state. Training is the means to arrive at this. When he has mastered the training, the training ceases to exist for him. This is the supreme aim of all the Ways.

Forgetting the training, throwing away all minding about it so that I myself have no idea about it – to reach that state is the peak of the Way. This state is passing through training till it ceases to exist.

KNOW THAT THE GATE SHOWS THE WAY TO THE HOUSE

Much learning is the gate for the beginner. What is meant is that you always go through the gate first, before entering the house, so the gate shows the way to reach the house. Passing through the gate and entering the house in the proper way, one meets the owner of the house. Learning is the gate to reach the Way, and through this gate one reaches it. But it is the gate and not the house. Do not see the gate and think it is the house. The house is something which is reached by passing through and going beyond the gate.

FALSEHOOD BECOMES TRUTH

Outer-and-inner is the basis of strategy. The real outer-and-inner is where someone is wary of it, and yet when it begins to operate, cannot get out of it. When my strategy goes into effect, the enemy is taken in by it. So it is winning by taking him in. When I see he is not taken in, I have something further, so that his refusing the first trap takes him into a second.

In Buddhism there is what is called hoben (indirect means). Truth is concealed and a provisional view is put forward on the outside; this does finally lead the pupil to the real truth, so 'false becomes true'. In Shinto there is the secret truth of the gods, and knowing that there is this hidden truth increases the people's faith. When there is faith, life has meaning. In the knightly arts, it is called strategy. Though this is a deceit, by that deceit society is preserved, and at the time of victory deceit finally becomes truth. Order is established by means of its opposite.

ACTION AND WAITING

Action (ken) means with one single thought to go to strike him down ruthlessly, or to run him through. This feeling of ken is the same in his heart as in one's own.

Waiting (tai) means not to move to strike at once, but to wait for him to take the initiative. It must be a state of utmost alertness. Ken-tai means the pair, action and waiting.

There are the principles ken and tai in both body and sword. When the body comes to close range, it is ken in the body while the sword is tai; by one's body, legs and hands one moves to tempt the opponent to take the initiative, and this is winning by letting him have the lead. Here the body and its limbs are ken and the sword is tai. To use the body alone in ken is for the purpose of getting the opponent to attack.

There are the principles ken and tai in mind and body. The mind should wait while the body attacks. For if the mind attacks, it becomes over-excited. The mind should be held back in tai, with the body in ken, and victory thus is won by letting the enemy attack. If the mind attacks with the thought 'Let me get him first', it invites defeat.

But in another sense one can regard the mind as attacking and the body as waiting. For the mind is kept ever watching, with the ultimate attack in view, while the sword waits in inactivity, to get the opponent to take the initiative. When it is said that the body is waiting, this is to be taken as simply the hands holding the sword. When it is said that the mind is attacking and the body waiting, it comes in the end to the same thing as before – to win by getting the enemy to make the first attack.

There is a Zen saying, 'the great action is direct and knows no rules'. 'Direct' means that the action of a man of full inner awareness appears directly; and the fact that the action of a man of such awareness is not bound by any of the training principles he has learned, or by any established ways of doing a thing, is expressed by the words 'knows no rules'. The 'rules' are the training, the ways of doing, the accepted methods. For everything there are instructions, there are ways and means which are usual. But the man who has attained gives them up altogether. He acts freely and spontaneously. He who is free, outside the rules, is called a man of great awareness and great action.

Awareness means never to lose inner clearness, to see in everything its real point. If this awareness congeals and grows hard by thinking and thinking, it becomes caught up in the things. This means it is not yet mature. But if practice is continued rightly, in time the awareness will become mature and fill the body, and he will work in freedom. This is called the great action.

There is a verse of Manorhita, the twenty-second Zen patriarch in India:

> The mind turns in accordance with the ten thousand things;
> The pivot on which it turns is verily hard to know.

This verse contains a secret of training. It embodies a central point of ways of attack and defence (Heiho) and so it is quoted here, but those who are not training in a tradition will find it hard to understand.

In attack-and-defence, it is the various moves of the opponent that are the 'ten thousand things'. At each one of them, the mind turns. For instance, if he whirls his sword up, the mind turns to that sword movement; if he turns to the right, the mind turns to the right, and if to the left, the mind turns to the left. This is what is meant by 'turns in accordance with the things'. Then 'the pivot on which it turns is verily hard to know' – to find this is the object of training. One must understand that this is a state where the mind leaves no track behind it, like a moving ship whose wake quickly disappears. If the mind keeps on turning and never stops at all, its track vanishes.

'Hard to know' means that it is not clear, that it is difficult to make out. The sense is that there the mind is not fixed.

If the mind does become set on one place, that means defeat; if in its moving it leaves something behind, that is still very poor. Mind has no colour or form and can never be seen by the eye; but when it sticks and becomes set, then it becomes visible. It is like white silk, which if it stays reflecting something red, becomes red itself; if it stays reflecting purple, it becomes as purple. The human mind too, when it reflects things, is seen in that particular appearance. If it reflects on beautiful youth, other people soon notice it. The thought is within but the aspect of it appears outwardly.

Heiho is in accord with Buddhism, and there are many points in common with Zen; one of them in particular is, not sticking to things, not setting the mind on a thing. Both of them cherish this not-setting the mind as a central point. In the play *Eguchi* the courtesan makes a verse in answer to the wandering poet Saigyo, who has in his verse protested against her refusing him lodging on his journey:

> It is only that I am thinking that a monk who has
>   renounced home,
> Should not *set* his mind on any lodging-place.

In attack-and-defence one must penetrate deeply into the meaning of this last line. Whatever secret tradition a man has trained in, if when he comes to use one of its techniques his mind becomes *set* on that technique, it means defeat for him. Neither on what the opponent is doing, nor on what one is doing oneself, nor on cutting, nor on thrusting – the main point is to practise not allowing the mind to be *set* on any of them.

ZEN AND THE WAYS

Songs of the Way of the Spear

HOZOIN SCHOOL (ABOUT AD 1600)

By what I did yesterday, I win today;
    This is the virtue of practice.

Remember the old saying,
    The plan for a day is a cock's crow,
The plan for a life
    is something serious.

In the knightly arts, first see that you yourself are right,
    And after that think of defeating an opponent.

The unskilled man does not know his own faults.
    And yet dreams vainly of defeating another.

The Way is first of all about one's own defects;
    After that, you can defeat others.

Without knowing the stains and faults in one's own self,
    How empty to dream of victory over others!

In the knightly arts, if a man's will is right
    There is no doubt of his ultimate victory.

Don't think to win just by force;
    There is hard in the soft, soft in the hard.

'Softness is just weakness', some say;
> But know there is a difference between softness and weakness.

When making an attack, do not be careless;
> There is a waiting in action, an action in waiting.

In all the turns of the combat, never must one get controlled by the enemy –
> This is what is always to be remembered.

In a contest, you must be aware of the distances and the timing;
> But do not lose sight of the awareness which is beyond them (zan-shin).

When you penetrate deep to the simple awareness (zan-shin)
> You will experience the state of being and non-being.

It is like a stream, which when flowing is pure;
> If it stands still, it becomes putrid.

Against a strong opponent, though you lose still you get something out of it;
> Do not think always in one straight line.

In a contest, first control your own mind;
> Only after that think about technique.

If you have control of your mind, be careful not to lose it;
    Hold the mind firm, and then make the thrust.

The hands waiting, the feet active without flagging;
    Let the heart be that of a waterbird swimming.

When the short body and the long spear are a unity,
    The enemy finds no opening to strike.

SABURI SCHOOL (SEVENTEENTH CENTURY)

There is no village where the moon does not shine,
    But it is clear in the hearts of the men of poetry.

Though one think, 'I have thrown away the world, my
    body is naught'
Still when the snow falls, the night is cold.

The samurai who is gentle in his benevolence
    and in his duty and in his bravery,
He is not burnt up in fire nor drowned in water.

Though a man is well equipped and strong and great,
    If he does not know the Way of the knight, he is as a
    stick or stone.

The beach pine has no voice;
    When the wind blows, it sings.

The water does not think of giving it lodging
Nor the moon of lodging there
    How clear the reflection!

The heart which can hear the frost forming on a cold
    night,
    When confronted with an enemy, will snatch the
    victory.

KAGOSHIMA SCHOOL

In blind darkness (mu-myo, the technical Buddhist term
    for ignorance)
    The rising and setting of the moon
    No man knows.

On the surface of Sarusawa Lake the mist is thick.
    What is floating and what sinking
    No man knows

A   UM
Study the natural state of the heart;
    Study it well to the limit of the two characters
    A and UM.
The two characters A UM are killing and saving in the
    palm of the hand;
    At the instant of being and non-being, life and death,
    you rise

To the peak of three thousand lives and deaths.
One glance, and you attain freedom.

If the transparent (white) dewdrop of the self
    Is put on a red maple leaf,
    It is a ruby.

TENTO SCHOOL

    It is vulgar to despise the other traditions.
        The Buddha in every temple is to be revered.

    In the shade of the evening, do not walk talking loudly
        and carelessly.
        Is there someone lying in wait?

    Don't argue about who does well and who badly;
        Seek where you yourself fall short.

Itto School
(late sixteenth century)

A verse of a master of our school:

> Unaware of the wind blowing in high heaven,
> The sheltered clover flowers yet know of autumn
> From the rattling of the shutters.

Question: What is the basis of our school?

Answer by the Master: As handed down traditionally, the basis of our school of swordsmanship is the Hidden Sword (In-ken; the In is the same word as Yin of Yin-yang).

This Hidden means that which has no visible form: it means the secret heart. Our school teaches manifestation of the freedom which lies hidden in heaven and earth, and is called In-ken, the Hidden Sword. In-ken does not mean cleverly hiding something which has a visible form. Heaven and earth do not think, do not calculate. Yet spring, summer, autumn, winter follow in due order, and all the transformations take place – it is like that.

The In-ken is concealed in the heart, yet when occasion calls, it manifests as the Wonderful Sword (Myo-ken).

Question: Are In-ken and Myo-ken both simply the heart, or is it that Myo-ken comes out of Inken?

Master: The word 'myo' does not mean some subtle stratagem of words or actions. In Buddhism it is said, 'The all-embracing wisdom of the three worlds, the Buddha-consciousness, is one with my own essence.

Now here in fencing (ken-jutsu), what has no form at all cannot be called Myo-ken. The basis of our school is the Hidden Sword, and the Wonderful Sword is then not to be seen; only when it comes out of concealment is it truly to be called Wonderful. In everything there is always the body of the thing and also its application or function. The body for instance can be compared to a lamp, and its function to the light – in a certain sense they are one and the same thing. In our school, the body of it is the heart-essence, and since that essence has no form, it does not appear as techniques and actions. So these are called the Wonderful Sword.

The ideas of attacking and defending are 'two', until the peak is reached. But when there is no discriminating or calculating at all, no idea of withdrawing, no idea of attacking, moving freely from the Gedan posture (the sword held low) to either striking or parrying, then there is victory. It is the Wonderful function when from that which has no form these manifestations of form appear in their perfection. Do not take technique to be primary.

Hard means rigid like iron, *soft* means pliable like the tongue and so on.

Strong is like a rock, *weak* is like a rotted cord.

Instant is like lightning, or as a spark from a flint, *fast* is like a man running.

Leisurely is at an easy pace, *late* is to get there behind time. Master Jukyo speaks of soft (ju) and hard (go), strong and weak in this verse:

Strong in their softness are the sprays of the wisteria creeper;
The pine in its hardness is broken by the weak snow.

and of fast and slow in this verse:

> We see no limbs on the rising sun, moving fast or slow,
> Yet it never fails to reach the west.

There are songs of other traditions:
> Don't try for victory by your strength alone:
> There is softness (ju) in the hard (go), hardness in the soft.

> Some say that softness is simply weakness.

Know that there is a difference between softness and weakness.

These pairs of words (hard, soft; strong, weak; instant, fast; leisurely, late) are all about the same thing.

When it is time for strength, apply strength; when it is

time for softness, be soft; to adapt to the enemy's changing moves is the way to mastery.

WAITING IN GOING-INTO-ACTION: GOING-INTO-ACTION IN WAITING

Master Jukyo has a verse on these:

> The difference between going-into-action and waiting is for an enemy.
> For myself, there is neither going-into-action nor waiting.

Master Chokai says: If you try to use going-into-action and waiting with the idea that they are two distinct things which you can do, then you cannot attain to what is meant by not making technique primary. How could you win? Even at the moment of going-into-action, let not your mind waver (from its poise); there is waiting in action, there is action in waiting.

The ancient (Chinese) classic says:

> If you know him and know yourself, then in a hundred battles you will always win;
> If you do not know him but know yourself, you will win half the time and lose half the time;
> If you know neither him nor yourself, you will always lose.

The old tradition says that your fencing posture is determined by yin and yang (in-yo in Japanese). [Posture includes way of standing, of holding the sword, direction of gaze and so on. There were many 'secret' postures to surprise opponents, and it was widely supposed that the best fencers all specialised in one or two of them.]

Now a yin posture is defensive, but it has yang (counterattack) in it; a yang posture is attacking but it has yin (defence) in it. So there is no posture which is specially advantageous or disadvantageous, and the old traditions do not recommend one. The posture should be one which gives play to the techniques one knows and which also conforms to how one feels.

Taking up or discarding any particular posture is inner freedom. The man who studies a special posture in order to get an advantage from it seems to be an expert on the outside, but there is always a hollowness within. His mind has been captured by the posture. In our school it is recommended to have the 'posture of no posture', so that there is no difference between the external and internal. One must practise to be independent of any posture. If a man makes the mistake of letting himself get caught up with some particular posture, he will win if things go as expected, but if something goes unexpectedly, he suddenly loses.

The way to win is not by (tricks of) posture, but by rightly realizing the spiritual principle (ri) and rightly expressing it through technique (ji). There are a thousand different postures, with their strong points and their weak points, advantages and disadvantages. That is why one must practise the posture of no posture. 'No posture' does not mean not to stand up at all – it means that when in a defensive posture one is not defensive, when in an attacking posture one is not (committed to) attacking. There is a posture, but when the mind is not fixed in it, that is called the posture of no posture. When posture and mind are one, that is perfection of posture. The posture then adapts to the thousand changes and ten thousand shifts and moves of technique, and this is perfection of no-posture.

A disease of technique is (to think that) the principle (ri) comes first and then the technique (ji), that the body moves first and then the sword. This comes about because one looks for ri and ji as external things. Technique must adapt perfectly to the changing circumstances, and it is not a question of first thinking and then making the move. When the ri-inspiration is spontaneous, one will change without thinking about it, will adapt without calculating.

Respect the changes which inspiration makes in oneself, without analysing them or calculating (their results). Success will always come when the heart is without disturbance.

One must recognise clearly the truth of what one really is. This is the aspiration of those who study this Way. Looking upward, with heart undisturbed by any concepts in it, he reveres the one undifferentiated Principle.

Let him practise his techniques devotedly without the idea of gaining something from them. As the calm water holds the moon perfectly, so let him not create disturbances in his life-currents (ki); and then all changes come from this one-ness. This one is altogether without form, like water which also has no form but adapts perfectly to the angles or curves of a container.

Let a man practise not that his body moves and then the sword, but that the sword moves first and then the body.

There is the instrument, the sword. At the back of the sword, there is technique; at the back of technique, there is the spiritual principle. The heart is the basis of technique; the body is the basis of the sword. To keep the basis unmoved and the instrument in front moving, that is fullness, the right way. To have the basis moving and the instrument lagging behind is hollowness.

Where there is fullness, success is certain; where there is hollowness, uncertain.

If there is an idea of some hoped-for gain behind the technique, how will the technique be able to adapt to unexpected circumstances?

Shin-no-Shin-To-Ryu
(Jujutsu school, late eighteenth century)

Some who have trained at fencing with wooden swords have worked out a trick of striking at the space just in front of the opponent's head (instead of squarely on top of the head in the orthodox cut). In this way they catch him with the very tip of the sword, and can make the attack from a little further off, with a gain in reach. But there would be nothing like this in actual combat. How often is an enemy despatched by a cut of only a couple of inches? And especially if he were in armour, he would probably not even be wounded.

It is well said that one should think deeply and train the heart, for the principal thing is the ri. When the enemy comes jumping at you, flying through the air like a bird, the spirit has to be perfectly controlled and the inner awareness wide awake, with the vitality brimming over to every part of the body. One must plunge into training before one can attain this.

What has been said about the secret tricks in kendo must be thought over carefully. It is not our tradition at all, nor does it help in grasping the ultimate Way.

A former teacher, Kumazawa, who was a follower of the Way, taught that the main thing is to train the heart, not to train in technique. This is the teaching of the masters, that the ri is a training of the heart. On this point our tradition is just the same as the tradition of that former master.

My own teacher used to explain a technique to us only roughly and then say: 'Now you have the root, and to complete the Way you have to train ruthlessly, crushing flesh and bone, for a long time, never forgetting that the basis of our tradition is mental training.'

Jujutsu is shinjutsu (the art of the heart, mental training).

For soft (ju) to control the hard (go), the first thing is to train to mature the inner principle (ri) in the right way. Hardness and strength are indeed most valuable in life, but people do not know how much to use. He who loves to dominate others, in fact ends up under the domination of others.

Force goes only so far, and it has a limit. It is not great when it arises, but great when it is fully committed. This is the basis of human passion. To discover means (ji, technique) for using force selectively, by first yielding to the other man and then using the lead so gained, is jujutsu. The most important thing is to practise ruthlessly; sleeping or waking, do not abandon control of the heart. First one specialises in technique till he comes to the end of technique and bases everything on the heart itself – this is the best way of practice.

Ki (vital energy) should fill the body. When it is aroused it is yang (positive), when it is quiet it is yin (negative). In our school we stress performing the techniques (waza = ji) by using ki, but ki is not something visible. If the body is defective in ki, the promptings of what is needed are not followed completely; though when seated in a correct posture the body may be at ease and relaxed and the ki-principle seems to fill it, when he moves to take up something, by the action his ki gets concentrated in one side of the body, and in the end the even flow of the vital ki is impeded. The secret teaching

ZEN AND THE WAYS

of our school is to cultivate the ki in the 'square inch' (just below the navel) and not to let the heart cling to outer things but hold firm at that point as the base. Then though in movement when active, or when sitting or standing, the basic ki is kept right and the functioning ki is quite free, so that when strength is put into the left side, the right side is not left empty of it, and when the right side is engaged, the left side is not left blank. And so with front and back.

Rising and sitting, moving and still, the even ki pervades all, and this is called 'immovable awareness' (fu-do-chi). A tradition says, 'While this is retained, there is success.'

The ki must fill all, and no part must lack it. Then it is full of functioning yet does not move; like a top spun by a child, though functioning in turning, it is as it were unmoving.

KITORYU SCHOOL OF JU-JUTSU

To win by securing the lead and not letting it go is the *lead-of-the-lead*.

When attacked by the enemy, to get the lead away from him and win is called *lead-of-the-reaction*.

The way of winning is not to be determined upon in advance. If one decided to try for lead-of-the-lead or lead-of-the-reaction, one's mind would get set on that, and if the mind gets set there is no right to a win. It may happen that it does win, but the timing and inner unity are precarious, and one should know that it is not the true principle of ri.

The Blue Dragon Stretches Its Claws.
When the blue dragon stretches its claws,
It withdraws the left one, and brings
*   out the right;*
The practitioner imitates this.
The hands are parallel to the ground;
the ki-energy is to be full.
His strength is put into the shoulders
*   and back.*
The whole is a circling movement,
*   withdrawing the rear hand past the knees.*
The eyes should look straight forward.
The breath is to be regulated, and the
*   heart quiet.*

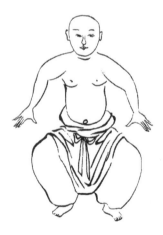

Three Plates Fall to the Ground.
The tongue presses firmly against the roof
*   of the mouth;*
Open the eyes wide, and breathe strongly
*   through the teeth.*
Now separate the feet and bend the knees.
Feel that the hands are powerfully grasping,
And then fling the palms out as if casting down
Something of enormous weight.
Now open the eyes and shut the mouth,
And stand up straight with the feet together.

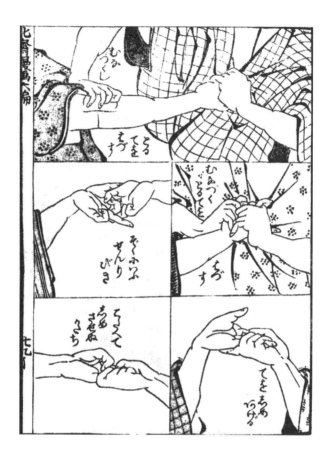

Hokusai. The top and centre right pictures show a jujutsu release; the centre left picture shows a finger lock which can be applied in cases where the opponent is gripping a cloth, to effect the first stage of a release. The bottom right picture shows a lock on the four fingers, which can be frustrated by bringing the thumb across and down, as in the left picture. This is one of the cases where the move is not technically difficult; in theory a mere knowledge of it would be sufficient. Nevertheless, in the schools this would be practised again and again, the purpose being to make it a natural action. If it has to be 'remembered, 'it will come too late.

*Above: an arrest from the rear. The left knee has probably given a jab
at the base of the spine as the man was pulled back. The attacker's right
hand goes through to prevent the victim from getting at his sword,
though in this case the artist has humorously depicted a totally
surprised man who makes no attempt to do so.*

Right: for this method of rope climbing the bottom of the rope must be fixed.

*Below: the technique of this throw is largely imaginary;
the artist is concerned to show the ki filling the
body down to the fingertips. (British Museum).*

Jujutsu formal exercises. The man on the left is practising the movement of freeing his right wrist from a hold by bringing his left arm over it.

The exercise on the right is practising stretching the limbs to feel the ki.

While both are sitting on the floor, the assailant on the left has drawn a short sword and caught the other man by the lapel to hold him while the thrust is made. The defender had retained balance and life even in an ordinary sitting position, so that he could rise onto knee and toes at once. He will pitch the attacker forward onto his face so that the weapon cannot be used. A tea master or musician preserves his balance all the time during his operations, as a trained eye can observe. The picture on the right shows a standing defence.

Okano Isao in contest. Note the loose wrist –
exceptional flexibility for a top judo contest (Kodokan, Tokyo).

Tengugeijutsuron

Translator's note

Most of the scrolls of the Ways are at least 80 per cent technical, and the theoretical presentation – such as it is – is overwhelmingly in terms of Zen. There are some other influences, for example from Shingon Buddhism and from Taoism, especially in the jujutsu schools; in the eighteenth century the Confucian element shows itself more and more strongly. In the eclectic Japanese manner, these various traditions are mingled and not felt to contradict each other on essential points. It must be remembered that in general the traditions themselves were tolerant; the Zen priest Takuan, for example, approved of the Confucian ideal for men in the world.

The Ways also were not regarded as necessarily distinct. A teacher of the Jigenryu school of the sword, which derived from (or was transmitted by) a Zen master, Zenkichi, at the end of the sixteenth century, taught etiquette, archery, horsemanship, the spear, the dagger, poetry and the tea ceremony. One of the earliest of the Ways was shooting from horseback, which dates as a specially studied art from the end of the fourteenth century. Fencing goes back to the middle of the fifteenth century, and jujutsu to the sixteenth.

It is interesting that the Ways of spear and of bow, in which the technical element is relatively simple and not capable of much development in the way of 'secret tricks', show the psychological side of the training most clearly in their scrolls.

The most fundamental Way, however, was taken to be fencing, and this was specially closely connected with Zen.

Seki-un, founder of one early school, took twelve or thirteen koans under Zen master Kohaku, and it transformed his fencing. Another fencing school based its ideas on the Zen instruction given to the founder Yagyu by priest Takuan early in the seventeenth century. Two of his letters to fencing teachers have been translated by D. T. Suzuki in his *Zen and Japanese Culture* (Routledge & Kegan Paul, 1973); the main points appear in the extracts already given here from the Heihokadensho classic, which was written by Yagyu.

In time, attempts were made to formulate a philosophy of the Ways independent of what some felt to be the otherworldliness of Zen. One such was a book published in 1730 called 'Tengugeijutsuron', which is a discourse on the inner side of the Ways put into the mouths of mountain spirits seen in a vision. The philosophy is the usual cheerful mixture, so that in this text one and the same word may have various meanings, according to which tradition was uppermost in the author's mind at the moment, and a single thing may be referred to by quite different terms. For instance, the changes of the seasons are said to be the Way of Heaven, to be changes in the universal ki, to be alternations of yin and yang, manifestations of the heavenly principle, or finally transformations of the heart. To a Japanese thinker of the time these formulations would not have been felt as necessarily contradictory; they might all be true on different levels.

The author's name was Tamba, but he wrote under the pen-name Chissai; he seems to have been an official who had a deep interest in the Ways, among which he classed academic learning, remarking that control of ki gives a new life to scholarship. He instances an experienced swimmer plunging into a flood, a boatman standing on the gunwale, a wood-cutter with his heavy load coming down a narrow mountain path, a tiler perched on the castle roof, as examples of masters of technique. If their hearts however are boiling with thoughts of gain and loss, or dull and apathetic, they are not on a Way, whereas if they are empty and bright, these men receive inspiration not only in their own craft but in other activities of life.

He approves of the Zen indifference to death, but rejects what he sees as another characteristic of Zen, namely indifference to the world and a certain carelessness as to what may happen.

Many of the Ways had developed technically in the peaceful seventeenth century, and to understand some of his points it is necessary to know that the teaching and practice was mostly in set forms. Some schools of jujutsu had a 'formal technique' (kata) of up to 150 attacks and defences, which were practised in a set order by agreement between the two partners. Some teachers believed that these 'forms' exhausted the possibilities of what could happen, and when mastered they would provide an automatic and appropriate reaction. The present work strongly contests this view, which the author compares to mastering the openings in Go, or the mating combinations in chess (some hundreds of them, incidentally). He emphasises an inspired flexible adaptation, creating something new transcending the traditional standard forms, and he condemns reliance on set forms, especially on certain secret moves which each school devised and then jealously guarded. For this reason I have avoided the word 'reaction', which has an association with automatic reflex action, the very thing which is so strongly rejected. This kind of automatic reaction takes place when the heart is full of other thoughts, and it is mechanical and predictable and hence can be used by the opponent to establish control over the other body as well as over his own. The 'wonderful adaptation' of the Ways, which I have translated mostly as 'inspiration', is creative, not determined by an opponent's movement though adapted to it, and it arises from vacuity and brightness in the heart.

Plucking a Star Out of the Dipper.
The practitioner stretches out his hand to the sky and feels that he is plucking a star out of the Dipper, leaving it a star lacking. He clenches his fist around the star and brings it down to his shoulder. (A mere instruction to stretch to the limit does not in fact succeed. These consciously created feelings, when they become so vivid that the hand tingles with the star in it, do produce a stretch far more complete than can be obtained by an ordinary effort of will, even accompanied by long practice. The long practice inevitably becomes boring without these poetic visualizations; the conscious efforts whipped up to overcome boredom in actuality lead to further contraction which inhibits the stretch. – Tr.)

Loosing the Shooting Star
(here from the right fist). A further form of the exercise
consists in stretching the other palm so that it is 'going
through the wall' – which must be felt in the palm. Suddenly
the clenched hand is opened wide with Fingers stretched,
and the star shoots as a meteor between the fingertips
of the outstretched hand.

Letting It All Go (Drop it!).

A noteworthy feature of the Tengugeijutsuron, which must derive from someone very experienced in a number of the arts, is the description of how an expert in technique can be rushed by an untrained man who is vigorous and carefree. This is something which ought not to happen, but which does happen, and it is vividly depicted in this text. It is also explained that if the technical expert can prevent his heart and ki-energy from being overborne by this sort of onrush, his victory is generally very complete.

The thought of Tengugeijutsuron is not systematically developed, and there are many repetitions of the same point. About half the work is translated here, and I believe all the main points are covered. Where there is an allusion which would be telling to a Japanese but would require considerable explanation for a Westerner, I have left it out. There are a few directions on the cultivation of ki by static visualizations, but the teachers of the Ways are in general rather against this kind of practice. They believe that after the very first attempts at tanden concentration, ki should be cultivated by simple movements, directed at a human end which is also a clear illustration of the inner process. Polishing, washing, cleaning, sweeping – anything where the true nature of a thing gradually appears during the process, are the best physical correlates to Zen training and cultivation of ki.

FROM BOOK ONE

Man is an animate being; if he does not move towards good, he will infallibly move towards bad. If *this* thought does not come up here, then *that* thought will come up there.

Something which changes in many ways and all the time is the heart of man. To have a realisation of the true nature of that heart and be in direct accord with the divine principle in its own nature cannot be done without a deep-seated determination to practise the arts of the heart and mature them. And so the sages taught their young samurai pupils at first mainly the six arts, to make them heroes, and from this training roused the search into the heart of the Great Way. When one has practised the six arts from childhood, he becomes master of himself and avoids vulgar talk; cheap amusements do not sully his heart, nor do negligence, prejudice, injustice or luxury endanger him. Outwardly, his sinews and bones are well-knit and he does not fall sick, and inwardly his character is of service to the country and he earns his salary. All of which is a help in the Great Way when the time comes to practise the arts of the heart. So none of the arts is to be despised as of no account, but nor should one mistake an art for the Way.

The sword is to cut, the spear to thrust – what else? Formal technique conforms to the ki, and the ki conforms to the heart; when the heart does not waver the ki does not either, and when the heart is made even and with nothing in it, ki too is harmonious and conforms to it. Then the technique is naturally appropriate.

But if there is something in the heart, ki tenses and hand and feet do not move as they should. When the heart dwells on some technique, the ki is checked and loses its softness. If one sets one's heart on forcing things, it makes no impression and it is a weakness: when one rouses the will to take control, it is like blowing on a fire when the fuel runs out. When ki takes the lead, it dries up; when it stays still, it freezes up.

If one thinks of concentrating on defending oneself and waiting, what they call playing for time, one inevitably stiffens up and cannot move a step, whereas the enemy can do what he likes. If one has a wrong idea of the 'waiting-in-action' and 'action-in-waiting' phrases, one's consciousness gets full of them and it is a great disadvantage.

There are many who plan to protect themselves by skilfully adapting (to enemy attacks), but when they come up against a totally unskilled but vigorous opponent, they are thrown entirely on the defensive and cannot make any counter-attack. This is all because they rely on conscious will. That unskilled man does not make any of the proper reactions; he has no idea of clever defences. With instinctive vigour and no nerves, thinking of men as no more than insects and without feeling he has to force things, he does not freeze or hold back, does not wait or hesitate. He has no doubts and no cleverness, just meets things as they are without thinking about them. Neither his mind nor his ki get caught up. From the point of view of ki, he must be ranked higher than some who are famous as experts in attack-and-defence.

Still, one cannot make him an ideal. Though he comes on like a rushing flood, without any check, this is a blind mushin, entrusting itself to the ki of the blood. The art of the sword ought to be inspiration in heart and body, without formal technique in its operation and without leaving any trace of its coming. When there is formal technique, when there is manifest form, there is no inspiration. Passing over into thinking even a little, ki assumes a particular form, and the enemy has a form at which to strike. When the heart has nothing in it, ki is harmonious and even. When ki is harmonious and even, in that living flow there is no settled technique. Without trying for strength, there is a natural strength, and the heart is like 'the bright mirror of still water'. With will or thought ruffling it even a little, the spiritual clarity becomes darkened, and cannot set itself free.

It is obvious that sword is to cut and spear to thrust, but to stop at saying that is to incline too much to the ri and neglect the ji. For a cut, there is a technique of cutting; for a thrust, there is a technique of thrusting. If one does not know how to apply the technique, one's handling of the things will be unbalanced. Though the heart may be strong, if the formal technique is wrong, the shot goes wild, and with ri alone apart from ji, one does not get the result one is supposed to get. My teacher used to call it 'clumsy grasp and vague speech'.

Even though his heart is 'illumined', to put a Zen priest as a general in charge of an attack could hardly be successful. Though his heart is not clouded with a mass of delusions, there is nothing he can do since he has not got the technique of how to go about it. Anyone knows enough to draw a bow and shoot, but if he has not trained in archery, real technique is lacking. If one carelessly draws and shoots, it will neither hit the target nor be able to pierce.

The will has to be right and the form correct, the ki filling and vivifying the whole body, without going against the nature of the bow. Bow and self become one. The spirit as it were fills heaven and earth; when the draw is full, spirit is composed and thought still, and the release is mushin, without thinking. After the shot, only the original 'I' having shot, quietly the bow is set down. This is how to practise the Way of the bow, and if it is done in this way the arrow will fly well and will pierce. Though bow and arrow are things of wood, when my spirit becomes one with them it is as if there was a spirit in the bow showing his power. This is not to be attained by conscious devices; one must already have a knowledge about the principle of ri, but unless there has been repeated practice of penetrating into the heart and mastering the technique the wonder of it cannot be had. If the will is not right within and the body not straight without, if the bones and sinews are not firmly knit, if the ki does not fill the body, one cannot by forcibly drawing the bow get a lasting grasp of any real technique. When spirit is not composed, nor ki lively, one cannot come to this Way by devices of one's individual will. When the bow is gripped and the string drawn by a forceful action, it goes against the nature of the bow, and bow and self are two antagonists. The spirit does not pervade it, and on the contrary its strength is blocked and its power lost, so that the arrow will not fly far nor penetrate.

...Even in everyday things, if there is no spirit of service, things do not go well. To go against the nature of the material is to oppose the natural feeling for it, and when one is separate and not in harmony with it, one is fighting against it. When the spirit is not calm there are many doubts and nothing gets settled; when thought is agitated, there is no inner peace and many mistakes are made.

What my teacher used to call 'bare energy' is called in some of the schools 'crushing', and it is a little different from the martial arts. It means to have no method at all, to overwhelm the enemy with a rush of energy, not avoiding strong points nor looking for weak ones, simply going straight for him and cutting him down, like a rock falling on him. But the man who does this does not have any method; he trusts to his instinctive vigour, and if he meets an expert in technique he gets completely trapped. Things are always uncertain, if one does not know the good and bad points of the standard forms. So there has to be training in these forms, awareness of defence and so on. And then, with ki not stiffened nor cramped, life and death forgotten, going forward with no hesitation, crush with the ki, crush with the heart. Both together. Unless heart and ki are one, he cannot be crushed. This is the best way of learning for the beginners in swordsmanship. But if the ki has some weakness, if there is even a little hesitation, it cannot be done. There is a training for ki, and a deep means to free the heart from hesitation. If ki alone is trained, one never experiences the inspiration of freedom to adapt, which comes from the heart-nature. One must devote oneself to the means. From long efforts in making the ri clear, when the sharp ki has been made even, in due time he will reach the essence. But if from the beginning he tries only the psychological means, he misses the real point and his efforts are to no purpose.

In the old days they had sincerity and goodwill, and were energetic in studying technique, never daunted or lazy. They had faith in what the teacher told them, and kept their hearts centred day and night. They tried out the techniques and together overcame all the difficulties. When the training ripened, they had a realisation of the self and its principle (ri). Thus their penetration was deep. The teacher, when he explained a technique, did not say all about it; he waited for it to disclose itself to the pupils – drawing (the bow) without releasing (the arrow) as it is said. It is not that he grudged it, but he simply wanted the pupils to devote themselves to it and so mature their training, putting their whole heart into it. When they attained something they would go to see him, and he would approve to the extent of their realisation, without giving any more instruction from his side. This was not only in the arts. Confucius said: 'If I hold up one corner and he cannot come back with the other three, I do not teach him again.' This was the old method of teaching. In scholarship and in the arts, they were indeed sincere.

But people today are shallow and indecisive, of little spirit, easily tired and lazy. They aim at small gains and want quick results; taught in the old way, none of them would train. Today the Way is opened up for them by the teacher, who explains the ultimate principle to mere beginners and tells them what to expect. But this taking them by the hand and simply pulling them along in fact becomes boring, and many there are who give up training. They look only to the ri principle and disregard the ancients, so while their practice is insubstantial they dream of ascending the heights. This is the influence of the present time. Instructing pupils is like managing a horse; its impulses to go the wrong way must be checked, but then it is merely encouraging it to go of itself in the right way, without using force at all.

When the heart is fixed on a technique, the ki sticks to that and is not harmonious. It is rightly called chasing after the branches and losing the main trunk. But to say one should disregard technique and not train at it is also wrong. Technique is the application of the sword; if the application is disregarded, by what means will the ri-inspiration manifest? By training at the technique, one realises one's true nature, and with that realisation the techniques become free. The true nature and the application have the same source and nothing separates them. Realisation of the ri-principle is sudden, but technique has to be ripened by training, otherwise ki stiffens and the form is not free. Ri gives rise to technique; the formless is master of the formed.

Those who practise today do not know the unfettered freedom of operation of a serene heart. They think to use conscious devices, and wear themselves out over the branches of technique, and think they have got something by it. So they have no understanding of any other art than their particular one. Now arts have many branches and to learn them one by one could not be done in a lifetime. If the heart truly penetrates into one of them, the others are understood without studying at them.

The beginner trains ki by means of practice of technique; if he sets out to train ki in disregard of technique, it is like a blank and he does not know where to turn. When training of ki matures, he will come to the heart.

How fast or slow it goes depends on the quickness or slowness of his nature. It is easy to know something about the inspiration of the heart, but to penetrate deep into oneself and actually have freedom in change is difficult. Swordsmanship is an art at the meeting of life and death. To throw away life and die is easy; to make no distinction between death and life is difficult. It might be thought that a Zen monk who has transcended life and death should thereby have perfect facility as a swordsman. The answer is, that the purpose of their trainings is different. The Zen monks want to leave the wheel of life-and-death for nirvana; they throw their hearts into the face of death, and shake themselves free from life-and-death. So among many enemies, though the Zen monk may be crushed by them, his thought is not agitated and all is well. But he has no concern with the application to life; it is only that he is not overwhelmed by death. This is not the same thing as the sage's 'one principle penetrating' life and death: living, to entrust oneself to life, dying, to entrust oneself to death. Without dividing the heart into two, following one's duty and fulfilling the Way, this is the freedom of it... The Zen monk is concerned with nirvana and not with how to use life. So it is only that he knows how to die well... But he is not free in making use of life. The teaching of the sages is to make no difference between life and death: in life to fulfil the Way of life, and in death to fulfil the Way of death. There is no will or movement of thinking about it: it is freedom in living and freedom in dying.

Question: What of the stories of fencers of old who met a Zen priest and came to realise the ultimate principle of fencing? *Answer*: A Zen priest teaches not the ultimate principle of fencing, but that when the heart is right it adapts to things, whereas hanging on to life only makes life a suffering. And he shows how the heart may be deluded about life, as if the three worlds were a dark cave.

When one has devoted himself many years to fencing, not really resting even in sleep or sitting, when he has been training his ki and mastering all the techniques, and yet he is still without inspiration in actual contest – months and years of frustration – now if meets a Zen priest and from him grasps the principle (ri) of life and death, and realises how the ten thousand things are only transformations of the heart alone, suddenly his heart is illumined and his spirit composed, so that he abandons all his hankerings and makes himself free. It is one who has for many years trained his ki and studied all the techniques who makes a warrior of this kind, and it is not to be attained in a moment. His long training in fencing corresponds to the training of a Zen pupil under the stick of the Zen master, and the realisation is not to be had while one is still busy learning the techniques. One whose art is still immature will never get enlightenment from the wisdom of even the greatest priest.

FROM BOOK TWO

Ri has no form, and its functioning is manifested through some instrument, without which it is not to be seen. The inspiration of the absolute appears through changes of yin and yang; the divine ri of the human heart appears through the four virtues. Though swordsmanship is techniques of combat, ultimately there is no perfection of technique without the inspiration of the heart-nature. But it is difficult for young warriors to attain it.

So traditionally the instruction has been in the nature of formal practice (kata), going through all the techniques of thrust and cut, attack and counter, lightly and without forcing them. In this way sinews and bones become well-knit, and the use of hands and feet is mastered, and how to use them in responding to changes.

While technique is immature the heart is tense, and one cannot move as one should. So the practice of the techniques is by 'feeling' (ki). The heart rides on ki to employ one of the techniques; ki, then, being the energy, is not to be restricted, but vigorous and untrammelled. When ri-inspiration is contained in the technique, the latter conforms to the nature of the instrument used. As technique matures, the ki becomes harmonious in it, and the inner ri-inspiration spontaneously manifests. When without any doubts one penetrates into the heart, technique and inspiration are one, ki controls itself, the spirit is composed, and the potentialities unlimited.

This was the ancient method of training in the arts, and it is the essence of that training. If technique is not mature, ki is not harmonious; when ki is not harmonious, it does not conform to the particular formal technique. Then heart and technique remain two separate things and there is no freedom of action.

FROM BOOK THREE

Question: What is it that moving does not move, and being at rest is not at rest?

Answer: Man is an animate being and cannot but move. When even in the many adaptations to ordinary affairs, the heart is not moved by things, the heart in itself, being without desire and without 'I', is at peace and composed. In terms of swordsmanship, when trapped by many enemies, engaged on both sides, yet determined to live and die with spirit composed, thought unmoved by the many enemies – this is called moving but not moving.

Have you not seen a horseman, how a skilled man gallops the horse east and west but with heart serene and not busied, with posture quiet and undisturbed? From a distance it looks as if the horse and man were joined together; he merely controls the horse's unruliness, but does not go against its nature. The man on the saddle is called the master of the horse, but the horse is not frustrated by him and goes willingly, horse forgetting man and man forgetting horse, their spirit one and undivided. One could say there is no man on the saddle and no horse under it. This is a clear example of moving but unmoving. The inexperienced man goes against the horse-nature and is himself not at peace. Horse and man always at odds, the man's body tense and heart busied with the horse's movement, and the horse fatigued and tormented.

In one of the texts on horsemanship there is a verse:

You force me forward, but when I try to go
You pull me up,
Catching me in the mouth so I can't move.

Here one who knows its feelings speaks for the horse.

Pushing Heaven and Earth Apart.
One palm pushes the sky up, and the
other, behind the back, presses the
earth down. The sensation must be
felt vividly in the palms, and then
in the shoulders. This heals
internal illnesses.

Drawing the Bow.
Squat down and extend the right hand,
one finger up. Pull with the left hand
very slowly, as if drawing a bow of
colossal power. Suddenly release the
left hand and fingers, as if an arrow
had been shot to the ends of the earth.

It is not only with horses, but it must be the same attitude when handling people. When you go against the feeling, and put your faith in little devices, you get flurried yourself and the others are confused.

... Little people, when they move, get caught up in the movement and lose sight of themselves; when they are still, they sink into inertia and cannot adapt to things.

Question: What is meant by the moon in the water?
Answer: There are different accounts of it in the schools, but it comes down to comparing the natural adaptation in mushin to the water and moon and the way the reflection comes about. There is a poem by an Emperor in retirement:

> The moon does not think to be reflected
> Nor the water think to reflect –
> The lake of Hirosawa!

At the heart of the poem is to be realised the natural adaptation in mushin. Again there is one bright moon-disc in the sky, and yet the ten thousand rivers have each a moon, it is not that the light is divided up among the waters. If there is no water, there is no reflection. Again, it is not that the reflection comes into being when it finds water. Whether reflected in the thousand streams or not reflected in even one, there is no gain or loss to the moon. Nor does it choose between waters great or small.

Through this, one should come to realisation of the inspiration from the heart-essence. The purity or otherwise of the water is not now the point. All analogies use something whose form and hue are familiar to illustrate something without them, and here the moon has form and hue but the heart has neither. Do not fret yourself by sticking too closely to analogies in every point.

It is said that ideally ki should be forceful and vigorous; but if one inclines only to use force without harmony he is inexpert in his actual application of it, and he who relies only on it, having no technique to go on, fails in his use of it.

Again, ideally application should be harmonious; but if it cannot command force and vigour, it flows but weakly.

Weakness and softness are not the same. Rest and slackness again are not the same. Rest does not let go the living ki; slackness is near to dead ki. Ki gets tied up when one cannot release it from the place where it has attached itself. It can be tied by thought. Negative (yin) ki again is tied naturally. In general, if ki is tied to some place, there is no speed in its adaptations. So a ki which is tied (yin ki) is late in applying a technique; when on the contrary ki takes the lead, its adaptation in technique is dry, nervously energetic (yang) but superficial. It is light, with no juice in it, and gets brushed aside like dried leaves before the wind.

Question: Why do the Buddhists reject conscious thinking as bad?
Answer: I do not know about Buddhist meditation, but conscious thinking is basically the functioning of knowledge and not a thing to be rejected. All that is to be rejected is when it is supporting the passions and going away from the true nature, taking itself to be all there is. Conscious thoughts are like the ordinary soldiers; when the general

is entangled in material things and becomes confused and weak, he loses his authority. Then the soldiers under him do not avail themselves of his knowledge but look to themselves alone, and pursue their private plans. And as each one is working for himself, the camp is in disorder, with riots and affrays, and in the end the army meets a disastrous defeat. When things have gone as far as this, the general cannot do anything; history shows that an army which is in commotion cannot be calmed down.

When thinking takes itself to be all, runs wild after sexual desire though it knows it is wrong to do so, there can hardly be control. The fault is not with the thinking. When the general is wise and brave, and his orders are clear, the soldiers respect his orders and do not go after their own devices. Following the instructions, they crush the enemy; their preparations are well made and they cannot be defeated. With the efforts of the soldiers, the general gets them a great victory. And if thinking follows the spiritual light of the true heart, knowledge and feeling operate by the divine principle; then the selfishness is not taken as everything, the operations of knowledge help the administration of the whole. Why should thinking be rejected? The compassionate thinking of the sage does not take itself as all, but knowing and feeling follow the divine principle in their own nature, and set a right course for the thinking. And this is called compassionate thought.

> The essential thing with the heart is to be clear and have no darkening.
> The essential thing with the ki is to be strong, vigorous, and not cramped.

Heart and ki are fundamentally one. If we speak of them as separate, it is in the sense of fire and fuel. There is neither great nor small in fire itself, but if fuel is lacking the fire cannot blaze up, and if the fuel is damp the fire is not bright. All the operations of man are the doing of ki. One of strong and vigorous ki does not develop illness, nor is he affected by the cold wind or humid heat. One whose ki is feeble becomes ill easily, and is oversensitive to an unfavourable atmosphere. When ki is sick, the heart is distressed and the body fatigued. The medical books say that a hundred illnesses arise from ki. He who does not recognise the changes in ki, does not know the source of the illness. So the basis is, that man should cultivate a vigorous and lively ki. There is a way to do this. If the heart is darkened, ki loses the way and moves out of control; when that happens it loses the power of vigorous decision. By using tricks, the heart's light is obstructed. With a darkened heart and the ki running blindly, there may be an instinctive energy of the blood but there is no freedom with technique, and even that instinctive energy of the blood is transient and without root. It moves without real effect.

The techniques of any field can be known by analogy with that of fencing. So a young samurai must fulfil his duties towards parents and seniors, and by so doing he subdues his selfish desires. When these desires are not running wild blindly, the ki does not stagnate, but serves the light of the heart with vigour and decisiveness. But when it is not vigorous, the techniques do not come off, and because they do not come off he resorts to conscious tricks, which darken the heart. This is called delusion, and it is the same in fencing. When spirit is composed and ki harmonious, the operation is mushin and the technique naturally appropriate – that is the ultimate principle. But first a vigorous and lively ki has to be cultivated. Unless there is a heroic spirit which discards all little tricks and overwhelms opposition, smashing through even iron walls as it is said, there is no ripening to the natural principle of mushin.

Merely of mushin, one falls into blankness; merely thinking of harmony, he becomes slack. It is not only in fencing but applies to archery, horsemanship and all the arts. Technique will not succeed unless first a heroic will and a vigorous ki have been cultivated. These things have to be known by experiment in oneself. Reading or hearing about them without trying them oneself is knowing from others but not being able to apply them. This is called second-hand knowledge. To experiment in oneself with all the techniques, whether of learning or of the arts, in the light of this principle, and to confirm it in experience of the heart, and so to find out the merits or failings, easiness or difficulties, of the various techniques – this is called training.

FROM BOOK FOUR

Question: Strategy and tactics are arts of deception by trickery. Will not a training in that way, with its little tricks, harm the training of the heart?

Answer: When the gentleman uses these things, they are an instrument for bringing peace to the land. When a small man uses them, they are an instrument to harm himself and injure others. It is the same with every technique. When the will is mainly concerned with the Way and no selfishness is involved, then even though he may be learning the so-called arts of a robber, the benefit is that he can defend himself against robbers and there is no harm at all to his will. But if the will is mainly concerned with passion and desire and profit and loss, then even books of saints and sages simply provide him with little tricks for himself. So first the will is to be set in the right way, and maintaining it so, he goes on to study the thousand techniques. If one goes to learn the fighting arts without the right Way being master within him, his heart is attracted by the fair promises of reputation and profit.

It is a mistake to think that skill in tricks is the main thing in the way of a samurai. If a swordsman when skilled in his art thinks that its main use is for affrays at the crossroads, then his art invites harm on him. There is no fault in the art, it is the will that is wrong. Kumazaka and Benkei were equally skilled in striking, with all the qualifications of fighting heroes, but Benkei used them doing his lawful duty while Kumazaka used them as a brigand. So it is not strategy and tactics which are the Way of the samurai; it is using them in the proper way.

He who uses evil against the right is a brigand. But to fight wildly, without preparing and without planning, and so become trapped by an enemy's plans, having one's loyal warriors wounded – would that be right? If I understand strategy I shall be prepared and not fall into the trap, but if I do not understand it, I become his prey. Is it good to be ignorant of it? It is true that strategy has many branches, but to put them into practice depends on human feeling. If they go against human feeling, one may know about them but one cannot apply them. Doctors read many books and know about many drugs, but if they do not understand the cause of the disease and give medicines at random, it invites a further disease. The general has to know human feelings, and unless there is the faith, the virtue, the benevolence in him, the human feelings (of his men) will not be in harmony (with him). When the human feelings are not obedient, plans turn out calamitously, as is clear from history ancient and modern.

Question: Just as I am trying to deceive the enemy with my plans, he is trying to deceive me with his. Why should there not be some one trick, known to me alone, which could confound everyone else?

Answer: What you say is the question of the standard forms. In Go and Shogi (chess), sequences of moves have been imitated from the old days, and it is thought that they have been completely analysed out and there is no more to be found out about them. But someone may come who is still more skilful. To learn the openings at Go, and the mating combinations at Shogi, is to learn these standard forms. But when one has got some advantage from one of them, some new move not covered by them suddenly turns up, and wins. All techniques in everything are like these standard forms, and in strategy too it is the same.

A general, if he has the ability, will come on some new flexible strategy, different from the standard forms, and this new thing will turn out to make the master strategists of the past look clumsy fools. There are many things which can be applied to the actual combat, and when the heart is attentive, everything seen and heard is a help to developing strategy.

But first one must master the standard forms of the past, or one cannot use the later developments.

It is the same with scholarship. Without having followed in the tracks of the ancients, one cannot come to know that Way where there is no track. All techniques always depend on the heart; everything one sees or hears should be an occasion for practice. At the time of using a technique, trust to the occasion. Again, in an actual battle when there are many on both sides, a single man can hardly act on his own initiative. What is necessary is always to think of what has been laid down by the ancients, train the men, and then be ready for flexibility in tactics.

Part Six
Stories of the Ways

READING A ZEN STORY

The following is a story which has been reproduced in several anthologies since it first appeared in my own *First Zen Reader* in 1960. I have sometimes heard it discussed, and it seems that many people miss half the point. If one is attracted to a story, it is proper to read it carefully, and find out whether there is perhaps more in it than the obvious surface point, important though that is. Here is the story. At the end of it a 'test' will be proposed.

A young man who had a bitter disappointment in life went to a remote monastery and said to the abbot: 'I am disillusioned with life and wish to attain enlightenment to be freed from these sufferings. But I have no capacity for sticking long at anything. I could never do long years of meditation and study and austerity; I should relapse and be drawn back to the world again, painful though I know it to be. Is there any short way for people like me?' 'There is,' said the abbot, 'if you are really determined. Tell me, what have you studied, what have you concentrated on most in your life?' 'Why, nothing really. We were rich, and I did not have to work. I suppose the thing I was really interested in was chess. I spent most of my time at that.'

The abbot thought for a moment, and then said to his attendant: 'Call such-and-such a monk, and tell him to bring a chessboard and men.' The monk came with the board and the abbot set up the men. He sent for a sword and showed it to the two. 'O monk,' he said, 'you have

PART SIX: STORIES OF THE WAYS   275

vowed obedience to me as your abbot, and now I require it of you. You will play a game of chess with this youth, and if you lose I shall cut off your head with this sword. But I promise that you will be reborn in paradise. If you win, I shall cut off the head of this man; chess is the only thing he has ever tried hard at, and if he loses he deserves to lose his head also.' They looked at the abbot's face and saw that he meant it: he would cut off the head of the loser.

They began to play. With the opening moves the youth felt the sweat trickling down to his heels as he played for his life. The chessboard became the whole world; he was entirely concentrated on it. At first he had somewhat the worst of it, but then the other made an inferior move and he seized his chance to launch a strong attack. As his opponent's position crumbled, he looked covertly at him. He saw a face of intelligence and sincerity, worn with years of austerity and effort. He thought of his own worthless life, and a wave of compassion came over him. He deliberately made a blunder and then another blunder, ruining his position and leaving himself defenceless.

The abbot suddenly leant forward and upset the board. The two contestants sat stupefied. 'There is no winner and no loser,' said the abbot slowly, 'there is no head to fall here. Only two things are required,' and he turned to the young man, 'complete concentration, and compassion. You have today learnt them both. You were completely concentrated on the game, but then in that concentration you could feel compassion and sacrifice your life for it. Now stay here a few months and pursue our training in this spirit and your enlightenment is sure.' He did so and got it.

Test: This man had been rich, but had never bothered to use his money to relieve the sufferings of the poor, whom he must have seen often.

Where did the wave of compassion come from?

Tesshu

Tesshu was a fencing master of the late nineteenth century, who had also completed the full course of Zen under the great master Tekisui of Tenryuji. An inquirer came to him asking for a discourse on the Rinzairoku classic.

'The Rinzairoku? Why, sermons are given on it regularly at Enkakuji; you'd better go and hear Master Kosen there.'

'I have been to hear him, but I still don't feel I really understand it. Now I know that you are an expert in fencing as well as Zen, and I have done quite a bit of fencing myself, so I thought perhaps it would be easier to understand if I had an explanation from you.'

'All right, then you had better change into fencing gear', and overruling the guest's surprise he made him practise fencing till he was pouring with sweat and exhausted. After they had bathed in cold water and changed, they sat facing each other as before in the guest room.

Tesshu asked, 'Have you got it?'

'Got what? I am here waiting to listen to you.'

'That was the discourse on Rinzairoku which you asked for. Zen masters in their temples teach it in their own way; that has nothing to do with me. I am a fencer and I teach it through fencing. You have had the explanation and that is all I have to give you.'

[Compare with the Sermon of the Nun Shido, Shonankattoroku no. 87]

Tesshu was famous for his physical courage and he carried out a most dangerous mission for the Shogun at the time of the Meiji Restoration. A young fencer who asked him about the inmost secret of the Way of fencing was told to go to the Kannon temple at Asakusa and pray to be given enlightenment about it.

After a week the man came back and said, 'I went every day and prayed for a long time but nothing came in response. But as I was coming away yesterday, for the first time I noticed what is written above the shrine: *The Gift of Fearlessness*. Was that what you meant?' 'It was', replied Tesshu. 'The secret of our Way is complete fearlessness. But it has to be complete. Some there are who are not afraid to face enemies with swords, but who cringe before the assaults of passions like greed and delusions like fame. The end of our Way of fencing is to have no fear at all when confronting the inner enemies as well as the outer enemies.'

Omori Sogen, a Zen master who is also a fencing master in the line of Tesshu, demonstrating Zen realisation expressed in a fencing pose.

Tesshu used to write out passages from the sutras every day and he continued this practice even during his final illness. When he could no longer do so, he invited a few friends round to the sick-room. They talked for a little, and then he said, 'Now I shall take my leave.' He sat upright on the bed in the Zen meditation posture, and died quietly.

As a leading fencing master of the time, Tesshu was asked to give fencing lessons to the young Emperor Meiji. At one of these lessons, as the two came close Tesshu threw the Emperor with a judo technique down on to the polished boards; this is permitted under the rules, but the watching Chamberlain was horrified at what had happened. Afterwards he spoke to Tesshu, and protested indignantly, 'It was most unexpected that you would dare to throw His Imperial Majesty.'

'Why not? It is part of what I am being asked to teach him. If His Majesty does not know what it is like to be thrown, he will not know fencing.

The Chamberlain did not know what to say.

All his life Tesshu remained a vegetarian in the Buddhist tradition. A busybody once came up to him and said, 'Surely from the highest point of view of Zen, to eat meat is the same thing as not eating meat?'

'Yes,' said Tesshu, 'the same.'

'Then,' went on the questioner, 'if it is the same, why do you not give up your vegetarianism and eat meat?'

'If it is the same,' replied Tesshu, 'why do you want me to change?'

One of his friends was a Japanese story-teller. In this highly developed art, the one speaker takes all the parts, changing his voice and demeanour so cleverly that the illusion of a world is created. His one fan becomes an umbrella, a sword, a cup, a pen and so on. Tesshu's friend was a master of his art, and he once gave a performance at Tesshu's house which was acclaimed by the audience as perfect. But Tesshu remained silent. Afterwards the story-teller asked quietly, 'Did you find some fault in my performance?'

'Only one fault.'

'And what was that?'

'That you have still a tongue.'

The story-teller meditated on this phrase for a long time in perplexity of spirit. It became a koan to him, and after a great struggle he penetrated into it.

He gave another performance, to which he invited Tesshu.

He was now not calculating his effects, but speaking and moving perfectly naturally. The effect was overwhelming. At the end the audience instead of applauding sat silent, and Tesshu nodded.

Disadvantages

A seventeen-year-old judo student who was very promising lost his right arm in an accident. When he recovered he began to go to the judo training hall again, and practise with the loose sleeve tucked into his belt. He could not throw anyone except a few friends who let him do so; when he told them to try hard his defences were completely broken, and he could not get near to a throw himself.

His parents consulted with the judo teacher, and they made attempts to interest him in something else. 'You have a fine judo spirit,' the teacher told him, 'and now you can use that spirit to excel in something where you don't need two arms. You might try table tennis – show them what the judo spirit can do in that.' But his interest could not be diverted from judo. This sometimes happens – for a time a particular thing becomes the whole world, and it was so in this case.

When the boy finally realised that he would not be able to make up for his lost arm, however much he practised, he fell into depression. He became unable to study, and hardly spoke. The parents again consulted the judo teacher who told them, 'I have no idea what to do. But we could take him to see my old master, who is a spiritually advanced man. He lives in retirement and it is a good way from here, but if I write to him I am sure he would see us.'

So the four of them went to the old master, who had been a contest champion in his time. He listened carefully, and asked a few direct questions of the son. Then he said to the parents, 'Is it intended that he should go on to university?'

'Yes,' they replied, 'but he is not studying now.'

The master was silent for a little. He turned to the judo teacher, 'What is the standard of the students' championship in your county what grade are the finalists?'

'Well, as you know we are a small county, but the judo isn't too bad. The champion is generally not more than Second Dan, but not under that either.'

The past master said to the boy, 'I can see that you will have to fulfil your ambition at judo before you can go on to anything else. Now – to become the students' champion of your county in three years' time, would that satisfy you?'

The young Judoka could only gulp in bewildered acquiescence.

'Then you must undertake to study again, because if you don't study you won't be able to be students' champion, will you? And I will make arrangements for your judo training, which you will have to follow without any questions or doubts. It will be a rather hard time.'

When the parents had finished making their thanks they departed with their son, leaving the younger judo teacher behind them. 'I suppose you think that I have been promising him something impossible in the hope that before the three years are over he will have got interested in something else? It could happen with some of them, but not that one. He will have to do it or die.'

'But master, how can he do it with the odds against him like that?'

'His disadvantage must be turned into an advantage. You remember how you used to have that bad habit of occasionally taking a wide step with your right foot? We reduced it by paying attention but still you occasionally did it when there was a flurry. When I realised it would always be with you and would come out from time to time, I made you practise Hizaguruma every day as part of your routine. Perhaps you thought I was being eccentric, or giving you something unsuitable as a test of your will-power? After all you must have thought to yourself that Hizaguruma wasn't at all suitable to your build. But it has been quite useful to you in contest, hasn't it? When you accidentally made that wide step, your opponent often automatically made a Kouchi attack, and then your Hizaguruma was all ready sharpened for the counter. So your disadvantage, your tendency to make a wide step, became your advantage; they used to walk into an unexpected counter.

'You have the principle from your own experience, but it's not enough to know *about* it. You must find some way of applying it to the present case. It will be good for you to train this boy, because the experience will turn you into a real teacher of the Way and not just technique. Now think how you are going to turn his disadvantage into an advantage. Come back next week.'

When the teacher appeared again he blurted out, 'I've thought and thought about it. All I can see is that this boy has got only one arm, and however hard he trains there will be others with both arms who train just as hard. You know some of them are just as keen as he is. I can't see how he can ever do more than put up a gallant losing struggle.

The master said, 'In your ordinary classes, train him in defence only. Even with one arm, he can get fairly expert at that, anyway enough to survive any rush attack at the beginning of a contest. Tell the other boys that it is a good opportunity for them to practise their attacks against someone specializing in defence. He'll take some hammerings, but that doesn't matter.

Then have him in private at your training hall every morning for half an hour. Teach him a few Jujutsu wrist turns which a man can do with one hand, and let everyone know that, so they don't get inquisitive. They'll think you're sorry for him, and giving him some special training in something he can do with one arm. And that will be true. But the main part of the time teach him some variations on Hanemakikomi and a special form of Osotomakikomi, which we can look at now.'

There are certain rare forms of throw which are extremely effective if the thrower can get in properly, but which are easy to stop. The defender just has to press with his hand on the attacker's arm, a small movement which can be made very quickly. To succeed, an attacker must make the complete movement with his whole body, covering a distance of perhaps two foot or more, before the defender can make this small movement of the hand. Judo men of any experience have an in-built reflex action of the hand to defend against this whole class of throws, and it is not worth while spending several years mastering one of them when it can so easily be stopped. Hanemakikomi is one of the rare forms of this class of throw, and it is hardly ever seen.

The one-armed judo student kept up his training on these lines for three years. He had a sad time at pure defence in the regular classes, and he had to work very hard in the mornings with the teacher alone, practising the movements until they were as natural to him as breathing. He was told he must never attempt them in public. As he got more expert, he often longed to score a few surprise successes against his regular opponents, but he managed to hold himself in. He had to put up with their pity, and in some cases ridicule.

After three years he was entered for the students' championship, to the puzzlement of his fellow Judoka. In the event he went straight through to become champion, winning in each contest in the first few seconds with a Hanemakikomi or Osotomakikomi. His opponents in later rounds saw the technique, of course, but found they were unable to check it in time.

What happened was, that when he came in, very fast, the reflex defensive hand action automatically functioned. But in this case there was no arm to press. This was a Judoka with no right arm. The whole system of defence reflexes became confused at the unfamiliar feeling, and the throw came off. Theoretically a defender could make some other defence, but at these high speeds no ordinary Judoka is able to modify his reflexes at short notice.

This is a striking example of the principle of turning a disadvantage into an advantage.

About 340 BC two Chinese states, separated by mountains, were at war, and the men of the Ch'i state were known to be poor on the battlefield. They appointed two generals to lead them, one being Sun Pin, descendant of the sage Sun Tzu who wrote the earliest classic on war. His colleague said to him, 'How can we face this enemy? Our men are not good fighters, and he is aware of it.'

Sun Pin said, 'Let us turn that very disadvantage into an advantage.'

He persuaded his colleague to lead the army through the mountains into the plain on the other side, and far into enemy territory. The instructions were to engage the enemy army when it appeared, but only briefly. Then a retreat was to be made, quickly and continuously according to a special plan. The baggage was kept to a minimum to facilitate this retreat.

After the first short clash the army went back quickly, just outpacing the heavily equipped enemy. On the first night, as arranged, every tent of Sun Pin's army lit its camp fire; on the second night only half of them lit a fire. On the third night it was only a fifth.

This was reported to the pursuing general by his outriding observers, and he concluded, 'I always knew they were cowards. Now their men are deserting in crowds. There is nothing left to fight.'

Sun Pin's men fled through a narrow valley, which the pursuers reached at nightfall. Knowing there was no effective opposition in front of them, these too went straight in. When they were strung out along the narrow defile, Sun Pin's full strength rained arrows and rocks on them from the vantage points occupied by the 'deserters', and the whole invading army was destroyed.

The man on the left sees that a dagger is about to be drawn,
and prepares to defend himself in the standard way against
the downward blow with the dagger, in the right hand.

But the opponent had in fact reversed the dagger.
His right hand came up holding the empty sheath. While the
standard defence goes into action, the dagger itself (held in the left hand)
has an undefended target. (Photos: Watanabe Kisaburo)

Endurance

In most of the martial arts there is a 'cold practice' in the middle of the winter when the students practise an hour or so with all the windows wide open. Some artists and poets do something similar. One poem composed on such an occasion was:

> Meditating that the Buddhas of the three worlds
> Are seated all around us,
> We do not feel the cold.

The chess champions have their own practice of endurance – it consists in the ability to sit motionless for hours together. I once watched the then champion Yoshio Kimura playing a championship game. He sat at the board like a statue, with his eyes half shut. His younger opponent was very fidgety – because there was only one move which Kimura could reasonably make. However, he did not make it for ten minutes. In the end his opponent became so irritable with these delaying tactics that he impatiently tried to force the issue and lost.

I met Kimura later, and to my surprise he was a fast-talking, wise-cracking Tokyo type, not at all like the priest-like figure at the Shogi board. I asked him, 'How is it that your Shogi personality is so different from your social personality?'

He made an interesting reply: 'When I was a youth, I played Shogi with an old master whom I knew to be inferior to myself. But he played very slowly, waiting a long time before making even an obvious move. I used to get impatient, and immediately he made his move I made my reply. But this only made him slower. In the end I used to try to force a quick decision unjustifiably, and so lost.

One day I realised that I should always lose to him if things continued like this. There was no way to hurry him, so the only means was to change my own impatience. I sat down and placed an empty Shogi board in front of me. Then I made myself sit there without moving for an hour, every day for a week. The next week I made it two hours, and then three hours. After that I could sit in front of a board, even during a game, without any feeling of impatience. Now I can out-sit any of them. *They* will lose patience before I do.'

I began at judo under a Japanese teacher of the old school, practising every evening till the training period ended. One day I felt rather off-colour, and prepared to leave early. The teacher said, 'Where are you

I replied, 'I am not feeling very well: I will come tomorrow.'

He said, 'If a man comes up to you in the street with a hammer, wanting to kill you, can you say to him, "I am not feeling very well; come back tomorrow"?'

I remained that evening till he sent me home.

This one remark, heard only that time but never forgotten, was a big help later on when facing very gruelling training programmes.

Inner archery

Early in this century a Japanese Zen master who lived in a temple in the country had as his pupil the wife of the greengrocer of a near-by village. Among his other pupils was a Cabinet Minister, who used to visit him once a week to sit in meditation for two hours and then have an interview. A newspaper sent a reporter to visit this teacher, and the pressman remarked, 'Why do you waste yourself in a remote place like this? Wouldn't it be better to come near the capital? Then instead of the greengrocer's wife, you could have more pupils like the Cabinet Minister.'

In his article, the reporter described ruefully how the teacher had scolded him for this remark. 'It is not a question of being the greengrocer's wife or being a Cabinet Minister, but of *not* being a greengrocer's wife and *not* being a Cabinet Minister. We teach archery here. She has to shoot herself out of being the greengrocer's wife into the Buddha-nature which she really is, and he has to shoot himself out of being a Cabinet Minister into the Buddha-nature which he really is. And it may very well be,' added the master, 'that it will be easier for her to shoot herself out of being "only the greengrocer's wife" than it will be for him to shoot himself out of being "His Excellency the Cabinet Minister". '

In the nineteenth century, merchants were not highly regarded; in particular it was thought that they lacked spirit. Some of them naturally resented this and sought to prove to themselves that it was not so. One merchant of the time took lessons at a school of the martial arts in what was then called torite, mainly methods of disarming and arresting an assailant. He made remarkable progress, and finally took the degree of chudan, which represented an expert skill in the art.

One night, a thief broke into the merchant's house. Brandishing a knife he demanded money. The merchant refused. The thief, who was a down-and-out samurai, came at him in a fury: 'What, a rat of a merchant standing up to me! I'll rip you open!'

At the words 'rat of a merchant', the householder broke into a sweat. His knees trembled, and he was about to ask for mercy.

Then his wife said, 'You're not a merchant, you're a chudan of torite.'

Suddenly he felt his body straighten up and his legs full of energy. He jumped at the thief, disarmed him, and threw him out of the house.

Teaching methods

There are numerous stories concerned with a man – perhaps a farmer – completely ignorant of fencing who has to fight a duel against an expert. He consults with a master of the Way, a retired fencer, who tells him what to do. In many of the stories the master tells him that he must make up his mind that he has no chance of saving his own life; the best he can do is kill his adversary at the same time. He makes the farmer sit and meditate on this for some time, until at last the latter says, 'I am resolved now – there's no escape for me, and all I want to do is to preserve honour by taking his life for mine.'

Then the master goes with him to the courtyard where the duel is to be fought the next day. The master looks for some distinctive mark on the ground, say a small reddish patch, and points it out to the farmer. 'Tomorrow arrive early and take up your position here, with your left foot on this patch. This is your starting point. You will be facing the sun and he won't object – he will be smiling at your ignorance. I'm not going to show you how to hold the sword – take it up any way you like. Now I stand a little distance in front of you, and I want you to watch me and imitate exactly my movements.'

There is a certain risky coup in Japanese fencing, which depends on taking two very large steps – almost leaps – quickly and without any hesitation. It means passing right under the threat of the opponent's sword, and even fairly experienced fencers sometimes fail in their attempt because inner tension makes them hesitate and also shorten the steps. In practising this coup, a student often *feels* that he is making wide steps, but an expert onlooker sees that in fact they are short. The fear of coming in right under the other sword contracts the muscles and inhibits free movement. The action itself is not difficult; what is difficult is to make it without any hesitation and to keep the steps very long.

The farmer soon learns to make the move, and the teacher gets him to lengthen the steps more and more. Now the master stands with his left foot on the reddish patch. He makes the two strides himself like lightning, giving a tremendous shout, as his sword swishes in the final cut. He says, 'You saw that my feet trod on these two places in the ground. I am now going to press two pebbles into the earth on the exact spots. Those places are charged with my power. Try now a few times – bring your feet on to those pebbles and make the cut in a single movement. Tread on the same places as I did and you will feel my power; make the same cut as I did and you will feel my power; give the same shout as I did and you will feel my power. Now try . . . you feel the power, don't you! Tomorrow, do that. He will be a man standing on a little rock in front of a mighty wave. His sword may cut it, but it knocks him off the rock and he is drowned.'

The next day when the referee gave the signal, the farmer leapt forward with a tremendous shout, and his startled opponent was unable to react in time.

There are many such stories, but it is not sufficient merely to know them. Intellectual people tend to write off such things as psychological tricks, suggestions which are 'untrue, but give confidence – to those who believe them'. As a result they themselves get nothing out of it. All the time they are saying inwardly, 'All that talk about charging with power ... the teacher wanted to give him confidence, and it might work with simple people, but intelligent people can see it isn't true.' Anything a teacher says is neutralised by being 'interpreted' as some kind of psychological means.

This is a mistake, and those who persist in it make little progress in the Ways. What the teacher says *is* true, and has to be accepted as true. There *is* a literal transference of power from the teacher to the pupil through the pebbles, through the shout. In the tiny area of that particular technique, on that particular occasion, the teacher does transfer his power and skill to a pupil who has real faith, and who has given up the idea of preserving anything of his own. By putting his feet on the pebbles, by the shout, by the spiritual preparation, the pupil momentarily becomes the teacher; for an instant he actually feels the confidence and power of a past-master. It is a fractional manifestation of the Way.

Janken

A soldier has a battle to face the next day, or a student an important examination, or a sportsman an important contest. He knows there is no more he can do now; he should simply have a good night's rest. Yet he remains awake. Silly. Reason tells him that to worry about what may happen tires him and makes failure more likely. Yet in spite of all, he remains awake and in tension. Even his deepest self-interest, supported by reason and persuasion, cannot manipulate the streams of thought.

A second-best way is simply to accept the condition. An experienced duellist was sitting up with friends playing cards before the encounter. One of them said 'Don't you think you should turn in? Your opponent is already in bed.'

'Yes,' was the reply, 'in bed but not asleep.'

This may suffice when a man's concern is for himself alone, and when the other side has the same difficulty. But the problem will appear in other forms which cannot be shrugged off with a second-best.

Attempts to manipulate the mental constructs do not solve these situations because the surface problem is not the real one. Unless all the levels, and all the faculties, of the personality and its roots are brought into play, no real problem is ever solved. The classical koan riddles, and the koans which appear in daily life, cannot be untangled unless the whole personality is brought out on to them – thinking, feeling, will, and finally the courage to make a leap.

Some Western people tend to believe that thinking is good in itself: the more thinking, the better. It is the same attitude which feels that an athlete who is enormously active is somehow better than one who is relaxed some of the time. But in fact, one of the main secrets of physical achievement is to alternate muscular and nervous relaxation with energy bursts efficiently directed. Beginners at things physical waste most of their strength, and beginners at things mental waste most of their thought.

Rational conviction is only a first step. The nervous student before his exam is convinced rationally that he ought to sleep, but it is no help to him. In the same way conviction about spiritual truths is generally of little help while it remains simply a question of thinking or feeling.

A teacher has to find something which engages all the faculties of a pupil; through this he can pierce through to the depths. Consider this example: a young married couple were desperately poor, but by hard work and thrift, combined with some luck, they became suddenly well-off and then rich. It became necessary now for the husband's business associates and friends to be entertained, but the young wife had such a habit of saving that she could not bring herself to spend, and things were always skimped. It began to be a disadvantage to them, because they were getting an unpleasant reputation of meanness, but though she saw that logically they must accept entertainment expenses for the sake of the business, she could not bring herself to do it. Even when she did spend the money, it was obvious that she hated doing it.

A Zen teacher was asked to see her, and she told him, 'I know what you're going to say, and I agree with it up here in my head. It's just that I feel down here in my tummy that once we begin spending it'll all simply go pouring away and we shall be without anything like when we started.'

He said nothing in reply, but remarked, 'I have been told you are very clever at the janken game. I have always wondered how it is that some people can always win at that – can you teach me?'

Janken is a familiar children's game, in which two players shoot out one hand, either clenched as 'stone', or open as 'paper', or like a V-sign, as 'scissors'. Paper wraps and therefore beats stone, stone blunts and beats scissors, scissors cut and beat paper. So each one beats one other, and loses to one other. If the two hands come out the same, that round is a draw. The hands come shooting out in a rapid succession of turns. The one who wins twice or three times in a row marks up one point.

The outcome of a few turns is pure chance, but some experienced players are able to win consistently when playing against the same opponent. They work by intuition and find it hard to explain, but it seems that most people have certain habits which come out in a long run of rapid janken. Some people when they try stone and lose to paper, immediately change to scissors, apparently on the unconscious assumption that the opponent will repeat his paper with which he has just won. Others always change with each turn; still others tend to repeat the same thing even four or five times. An expert begins to have an intuition of what the opponent is going to do, and can regularly win over a period.

The wife was going to explain some of this, but to her amazement the Zen priest simply came out with stone again and again. She expected him to change occasionally, so

Janhen. (Atsuko Morikawa)

sometimes she made the scissors or the stone, and then he won or drew. But as he persisted it became clear he was not going to change; she produced the paper each time, and the game became no game. She stopped and explained,

'Your Reverence, it's no good always making the stone like that. You have to try something else or it isn't a game at all.'

'Oh he said, 'oh I see. Let's try again.'

Now he began coming out with the paper, and continued with that, so that he lost every time and it became ridiculous. 'Well,' he said finally, 'I can see that I'm never going to be able to master this game. Anyway, thank you for putting up with me, and now … and he took his leave.

When her husband came back she told him what had happened. 'They say he's so clever, but I think he's an absolute fool. You know he kept bringing out the stone' – and she suited the action to the word – 'and he went on doing it, on and on and on. And then I told him, I said, you can't win like that, you have to try another one, and you know what? he went on paper, paper, paper all the time', and she was laughing and holding out her hand in the paper sign.

As she held her hand out she stopped laughing and looked at it. She stared at it for quite a little time; then she clenched her fist into the stone and looked at that. She became lost in thought.

At the next party, the entertainment was on the proper level and she was really hospitable. Thereafter she had no trouble in entertaining generously when the occasion called for it, without falling into meaningless expense when not necessary. Through her favourite game she had learned that to keep the hand always closed will not be right, but neither will it do to have the hand always open. But one does not have to do either of those things; one can alternate them appropriately.

This story makes the same self-evident point which had failed to influence the young wife's behaviour in the first place. To tell it to someone else with that problem would have no effect at all. It would simply be another bit of 'advice'.

The reason it had an effect on this wife was, that the illustration concerned something which she had made a vital interest. She must have played the game a great deal.

It does not matter what were the deep-seated impulses which gave it such attraction for her: they were there, and she found a deep emotional significance in the open hand of the paper and the tight-clenched fist of the stone, because they had been often connected with excitement and tension and disappointment and triumph. The Zen teacher must have made inquiries as to what she was really interested in, and when he found it, he was able to make inspirational use of it.

It is necessary to see from this story that it is not much use taking up some koan or problem idly, wondering vaguely what the answer might be while knowing that it doesn't in the end matter whether one hits or misses. The original koan situations mattered vitally to the people who went through them; there was a tremendous charge of vitality wrapped up in them. But to someone reading about them hundreds of years later, it is only like a chess problem or a crossword or wondering what will happen next in a television serial. A skilful teacher is able to invest the koan riddles with urgency till they become the whole world, but it may not be particularly easy even in a traditional environment. The teacher seeks for a koan, not necessarily one of the classical koans, on to which the pupil can bring out the whole personality, not merely intellectual curiosity or appreciation of beauty or mystery or simply exercise of will.

To some extent the teacher has to re-create the original situation; this may not be so impossible as it sounds, because there are typical situations which occur in most lives. But it takes time to invest what is at first merely a story with the necessary charge of actuality. One of the advantages of the Ways is that the situations arise fresh in living experience during practice of the Way; a possible disadvantage is that a pupil may think his enlightenment, so far as he gets it, applies only in the circumstances of his particular Way.

The rat

A fencing teacher on a journey visited a temple, and was given hospitality by the priest whom he knew. The food was served to him when he arrived, laid before him respectfully by a small boy who then sat on the other side of the room perfectly still while he ate. On the hot summer evening the sliding doors into the garden were open, and the master noticed a rat creeping stealthily in. The boy sat like a statue as it passed in front of him, then suddenly lunged forward, caught it and flung it out with one movement. The master went on eating with no remark.

Next day he asked the priest, 'Who is that boy?'

'An orphan', was the reply, 'whom we took in because no one would have him. He has no inclination to Buddhism; he is a very wild boy whose only interest is in fencing. He was thrilled to be allowed to bring your food.'

The teacher said, 'If he is willing, I will take him off your hands and train him.'

Ten years later, this boy was a good fencer, and he had a duel against a man whom he believed to be technically superior. He consulted his teacher to inquire whether there was any trick by which he might hope to win. 'That man knows them all' said the teacher, 'but think back to when you first met me and caught that rat. Did you think how you would set your hand on it?'

'No, I simply caught it.'

'Then do the same in your duel tomorrow; don't think of any particular way of attack or defence. The night before the duel you will not sleep and neither will he; spend the night meditating on the rat.'

The next day the duellists faced each other, and neither made any move for twenty minutes. This is a sort of psychological contest, in which the less experienced man loses patience and comes out with any special attack which he has prepared, without waiting for a proper opening. As it does not find an opening, it can be parried easily, perhaps countered; in any case the advantage of surprise is gone. The young fencer did not fall into the trap, because he had not prepared any special attack. It was his opponent who lost patience and made the first attack. He parried and countered with a thrust, which is a risky move. If it succeeds it wins right away, but if it fails it is often impossible to recover balance quickly.

He made the thrust and missed. The onlookers were expecting that he would be cut down before he could recover, but in fact it was the opponent who fell. He said later, 'When I missed, I knew he would get me before I could recover. But as I missed, I saw at his waist there was an ornament in the shape of a rat; the sword turned in my hands and skewered it, and he went down. Afterwards when I looked I found the ornament was not a rat after all. I don't know how the sword moved – it moved itself.'

Music

In the East the highest kind of music is that which sends the listener into samadhi. The silence which follows is an essential part of the music. The audience should be in the state of people who are watching the sun setting into the sea – they forget the circumstances which brought them there, they forget words like 'sun' and 'sea', they forget their own names and individualities. After the sun has gone, for a time there is no impulse to move – certainly not to clap or applaud.

A Far Eastern tradition says that Indian music derives from that played by the gods in the Lumbini Grove at the time of the birth of Buddha.

The ancient Chinese chin – a sort of horizontal harp with seven strings – is audible to only a very short range round the player. The chin has nacre studs set at intervals along the body, and the purpose is to enable it to be played in the moonlight, without any other illumination. The moonbeams make the studs faintly luminous so that the player knows where his fingers are.

Among the instructions to the player of the chin (which was one of the accomplishments of the cultured man) there is one which directs him not to become too interested in technical skill; he should avoid technically difficult pieces which partly aim at showing off dexterity. From the Far Eastern point of view there is a certain vulgarity in the emphasis on technical dexterity in much of Western music; in particular the device of the cadenza, which is often little more than an athletic performance without musical value or even relevance to the concerto in which it appears. The correlation of excellence with technical demands is a barrier to the ordinary amateur; it is unfortunate that in Western music as a whole, the best pieces so often contain passages beyond the range of the ordinary amateur. Sometimes these passages are few, but they still bar him from playing the piece as a whole. A new flute was devised in China, and a Japanese master flautist learned it while he was visiting the mainland. He brought back a number of the new flutes and the method of making them. He lived in the capital, but undertook performances in various parts of the country to spread the knowledge of the new instrument.

At one musical centre a long way from the capital, this master was introduced as the last item in the annual concert which the guild of musicians used to give. The master sat in the centre of a great gathering of musicians and music lovers, and played one melody on the new flute. When he finished he sat quite still, and the whole assembly remained motionless. After some time, an old musician said, 'Like a god!'

The next day, before the master left, the guild of musicians asked him whether he would take a pupil from among their ranks. They would together subscribe the sum needed for the training. How long would it be, in the case of one already expert on the flute? 'About three years.' It was agreed that they should choose one man to learn the new flute, so that he could come back and teach it to the others.

They selected a young man, a brilliant musician, and he set off for the master's house with the money entrusted to him, part the honorarium for the master, and part for his own living expenses. He made over the first on his arrival, and then set to work. The master gave him only one piece;

he practised it all day and played it to the master in the evening. At first he was given considerable technical instruction, but after a few months the master made no comment except 'Something lacking'. The young man re-doubled his efforts, but the comment was still the same. He knew he was technically perfect, but he could not return without the certificate of mastery sealed by the teacher. He was in agony, alternately elated by the hope of success, and then tense at the thought of the disgrace if he failed. He asked that the tune be changed, but the master refused to do it. After a long time the pupil gave up in despair. One night he slipped away from the house.

He could not face the guild without the teacher's certificate, and he took lodgings in the town. He tried practising other tunes on the new flute, but he felt himself that there was something still lacking, though he could not find what it was. He began to drink heavily and finally came to the end of his money.

He drifted back, as a semi-beggar, to his own part of the country, but was too ashamed to show himself to the musicians. They made no attempt to get in touch with him. He lived in a little hut well away from the towns; some neighbouring farmers who had heard his flute sent their children to him to take beginners' lessons. He still occasionally played on the new flute, but without being able to find any new inspiration in it.

Early one morning two messengers, came to him from the guild of musicians. One was the oldest past-master, and the other the youngest apprentice musician. 'Today we are holding our annual assembly, and we beg you, every one of us, to take part. The past has never been; there is only today. We ask you today to join us – we are all resolved that we will not hold our assembly without you.'

They overcame his feelings of shame, and in a dream he picked up his flute and went with them.

When they arrived he sat fearfully in the shadow of a pillar; no one broke in on his thoughts. As the last item of the concert, the announcer called his name, and in his tattered clothes he went out to the centre. He found that the instrument he had picked up was the new flute. Now he had nothing to gain and nothing to lose. He played the piece which he had played so many times to his teacher in the capital. When he finished there was dead silence. No one moved for a little time, and then the voice of the old past-master was heard in the still air, 'Like a god!'

The bell

This was when Ekido was abbot of the Zen temple Tentoku-in, in the nineteenth century. One morning he heard the dawn bell being rung and after a little he called his attendant from the next room and asked. 'Miho is ringing the bell this morning?'

The attendant said it was a newly entered boy. The abbot later called the boy and asked, 'When you rang the dawn bell today, what were you thinking about?'

'Nothing special. I was just ringing the bell.'

The abbot said, 'No, there must have been something in your mind. Well anyway, when you ring the bell, always do it as you did today. It was no ordinary ringing.

Then the boy said, 'I once heard that whatever we do, it must be service of the Buddha. I was told to meditate on the things as Buddha. So this morning I was thinking that the bell is Buddha, and that each time I rang it the Buddha's voice is sounding out. Each time I was making a bow, and I felt I was ringing it as a worship.'

The abbot said, 'That was a fine teaching that you heard. Whatever you do later in life, do it like that.'

This boy later became the head of the great Eiheiji training temple; his name was Dengo Morita.

The fortune-teller

Yagyu Munenori was a great student of fencing technique, and there was a standing invitation to any challenger to come to his house and have a contest with him with wooden swords. Afterwards Yagyu used to discuss fencing with the opponent over a meal; even if the other had lost, there was often something to be learnt from his techniques. There were many unorthodox styles of fencing which relied mainly on surprise, and it was essential for the teacher of fencing to the rulers of Japan to know about all of them. Some of the wandering swordsmen were wild figures, like the famous Musashi who used to dress almost like a tramp.

One day an extraordinary figure appeared to challenge Yagyu. He was very thin and held the sword in an unusual way. There were at the time two main styles of contest technique: to wait cautiously for an opening, or to rush the opponent with a continuous volley of cuts. This man followed neither; he advanced swiftly with his sword held almost straight in front of him in an apparently awkward grip. Yagyu however had met before a type of expert who relied on a lightning counter-stroke from an unfavourable situation, using exceptionally fast movement, long practised, to defeat the opponent's reflexes. He found the absolute confidence of this thin man upsetting; the man was taking tremendous risks, inviting a blow at the head as if saying, 'However fast your direct blow, my counter will be even faster.

Yagyu found himself giving ground more and more. When they reached the end of the practice hall, his opponent made a clumsy halfhearted blow at his head which he easily parried; Yagyu countered with a light tap on the head which the other made no attempt to stop. The contest was over.

At the meal Yagyu asked him who he was, and the other looked down and said, 'The fact is that I am a fortune-teller from a few streets away. I have had no customers and I am starving. I thought I would challenge you, suffer the pain of a blow on the head, but at any rate get a meal afterwards. But you didn't seem to want to hit me.' Yagyu gave him some money as well as the meal, and said seriously, 'I have surely learned something from your fortune-telling fencing.'

The pencil stub

An old lady in a country village brought up her little grandson, both of whose parents had died. She had little money and had a hard time doing it; the village were made aware of the extent of her sacrifices, and she did not have many friends. Living near by was a retired master of calligraphy, a man far advanced on the Way. He took an interest in the education of the village children, and told the old lady that her grandson was bright and should go on to a university.

When the time came he said, 'If you and he are willing, I will give you an introduction to the head of a university in the capital whom I know well, where they have a hostel for country students.'

The grandmother told him, 'Of course I shall be very lonely, but for the boy's sake I agree.'

As the calligrapher sat down to his writing table, she thought, 'Now I shall see something', but instead of a brush he picked up an old blunt pencil stub. With a tiny knife he made a couple of cuts to take away a little of the wood but did not sharpen it. Then he took an ordinary piece of paper and scribbled something in a very loose hand which she could not read at all. He did not seal it, but put it in an envelope which he addressed carefully and clearly. He passed it over and said, 'Show him that.'

The old lady was overcome with embarrassment; she thought, 'How can I just show up a scribble like that, not even sealed? Anyone could have written it. The principal will probably refuse even to see me.' But there was no help for it, so she accepted the tickets to the capital and they went. She presented the note to the secretary of the university president, who saw them at once. He was looking at the piece of paper as they went in, and after the introductions he remarked, 'What a wonderful piece of writing! Who else could have done it? He is using a blunt pencil, and he has such control that he can vary the pressure to imitate a brush stroke. I will certainly make arrangements for a pupil recommended by him – and I should like to keep this note, which is a masterpiece.'

She was now alone during the term times, but it turned out that she was not so lonely as she had expected. More and more people began to drop in to her little house for a talk, bringing some present with them. One day one of them said, 'Do you know why people like me call on you? In the old days you used to complain a lot and we found it rather tiring to listen to. But now you never complain, in fact you don't say much at all. But when we go away from here, we find we have a sort of strength, a courage to face life. I am saying this only because I want to ask what made the change in you.'

The grandmother told her the story of the pencil, and said, 'Afterwards I found that all the time I was asking myself, Why did he do it? It was like a puzzle that I couldn't get out of my mind. He had all those brushes, and I know some of them are very rare ones which come from some place in China. But he used that old pencil stub, and still the university president said it was a masterpiece. He asked if he could keep it, you know. I thought and thought; I was always thinking, the pencil, the pencil. And that went on quite a time. One morning when I woke up it suddenly came to me, I am the pencil. My life is a worn-out stub, my body is dull and my mind blunt. But with just one or two little cuts, cutting away my selfishness, the Buddha can use it to write a masterpiece. That was the thought that came then – the Buddha can write a masterpiece. Since then I have felt a strength holding me, and peace within.'

Historical Appendices

1.   Imai Fukuzan's introduction to Shōnankattōroku

The origin of warrior Zen in Kamakura, and in the whole of the eastern part of Japan, goes back to the training of warrior pupils by Eisai (Senkō Kokushi). But it was the training of warriors and priests by two great Chinese masters, Daikaku and Bukkō, which became the Zen style of the Kamakura temples. There were three streams in Kamakura Zen:

scriptural Zen;
on-the-instant (shikin) Zen;
Zen adapted to the pupil (ki-en Zen).

Scriptural Zen derives from Eisai, founder of Jufukuji in Kamakura in 1215, and of Kenninji in Kyōto. But at that time it was rare to find in Kamakura any samurai who had literary attainments, so that the classical kōans from Chinese records of patriarchs could hardly be given to them. The teacher therefore selected passages from various sūtras for the warriors, and for monks also. These specially devised scriptural Zen kōans used by Eisai at Kamakura numbered only eighteen, and so the commentary to the Sōrinzakki calls Jufukuji 'temple of the eighteen diamond kōans'. However, after Eisai, his successors in Kamakura of the Ōryū line (to which he belonged – the founder died in China in 1069 and the line was dying out there when it was brought across by Eisai) soon brought them up to one hundred scriptural kōans, to meet the various temperaments and attainments of their pupils. These successors were Gyōyū, Zōsō, and Jakuan at Jufukuji; Daiei, Kohō, Myōō at Zenkōji; Sozan, Gakkō at Manjuji, and others.

Among these augmented scriptural kōans were passages from the sūtras but also from the sayings of the patriarchs, to suit the depth or shallowness of comprehension of pupils, whether monks or laymen. Thus the warriors who applied for Zen training in Kamakura in the early days studied both the Buddha Zen (nyorai Zen) and the patriarchal Zen, but it can be said that those who were given classical kōans from the Hekiganshū or Mumonkan and so on would have been extremely few. From the end of the sixteenth century, however, the teachers did begin to rely mainly on stories from the records of the patriarchs, for training both monks and laymen. Kamakura Zen now gradually deteriorated, and by about 1630 no printed text of the Shōnankattōroku existed, but only manuscript copies. Some time towards the end of the seventeenth century, a priest named Tōan in Izumi selected ninety-five of the (Kamakura) scriptural kōans, and got a friend, a priest named Sōji, to have them printed as a twovolume work entitled Kyōjōkōanshū (anthology of scriptural kōans). These ninety-five correspond to the Kamakura scriptural kōans, though with five missing (two from the Diamond Sūtra, one from the Kegon Sūtra, one from the Lotus Sūtra and one from the Heart Sūtra). This book still existed in 1925.

On-the-instant Zen (shikin-Zen, sometimes read sokkon-Zen) arose from the training of warriors by Daikaku, first teacher at Kenchōji. He had come to Japan in 1246, and had been briefly at Enkakuji of Hakata city in Kyūshū, and then

ZEN AND THE WAYS

at Kyōto; while his Japanese was still imperfect, and without taking time to improve it, he came to Kamakura. Thus this teacher had to be sparing of words, and in training pupils he did not present them with classical kōans about Chinese patriarchs which would have required long explanations of the history and circumstances of the foreign country; instead he made kōans then and there on the instant, and set them to the warriors as a means to give them the essential first glimpse. Bukkō Kokushi, founder of Enkakuji, arriving in Japan on the last day of the sixth month of 1280, came to Kamakura in the autumn of the same year, so that he too had no time to learn Japanese but began meeting people straight away. He also had to confine himself to speaking only as necessary, and in the same way made kōans for his warrior pupils on the spur of the moment. Thus at both these great temples there was what was called 'shikin' or on-the-instant Zen. Before Daikaku Came to Japan, something of the true patriarchal Zen had been introduced by such great Zen figures as Dōgen and Shōichi (Bennen), but monks and laymen were mostly not equal to it and many missed the main point in a maze of words and phrases. Consequently Bukkō finally gave up the use of classical kōans for Zen aspirants who came to him in Kamakura, and made them absorb themselves in things directly concerning them. The Regent Tokimune himself was one of the early pupils in this on-the-instant Zen, and he was one who grasped its essence.

Zen adapted to the pupil meant, at Kamakura, making a kōan out of some incident or circumstance with which a monk or layman was familiar, and putting test questions (satsumon) to wrestle with. It would have been very difficult for the Kamakura warriors, with their little learning, to throw themselves at the outset right into the old kōan incidents in the records of the patriarchs. So in the Zen temples of Kamakura and of eastern Japan generally, the style was that only when their Zen had progressed somewhat did they come under the hammer of one of the classical kōans.

Among the old manuscript books in Kanazawa and Nirayama libraries there are many concerning Kamakura Zen, for instance Nyūdōsanzenki, Gosannyūdōshū and so on. But it is only the Shōnankattōroku which has a commentary with details of when each kōan began to be used as such, and in which temple, and also discourses and sermons on them.

In the tenth month of 1543, a great Zen convention was held at Meigetsuin as part of the memorial service, on the 150th anniversary of the death of Lord Uesugi Norikata, its founder. Five hundred printed copies of the Shōnankattōroku were distributed to those attending. The book included sermons on the kōans by Muin, the rōshi of Zenkōji. The work consisted of a hundred kōan stories selected from Gosannyūdōshū and other texts, by Muin Rōshi, as particularly suited to the warriors whom he was training at the time. With the decline of Kamakura Zen at the end of the sixteenth century, the copies of this book disappeared and it became extremely difficult to find one. What remained in the temples were almost entirely manuscript copies.

In 1918 I examined the old records at Kenchōji in the four repositories of the sub-temples of Tengen, Ryūhō, Hōju and Sairai, and among the stacks of old books there were some seventeenthcentury manuscript copies of the Shōnankattōroku, but all had pages missing from the ravages of worms, and it was barely possible to confirm from part of the contents that they had all been copies of one and the same book. In the first years of Meiji, Yamaoka Tesshū was given a copy by the Zen priest Shōjō of Ryūtaku temple in Izu, and he allowed Imai Kidō to make a further copy of it.

In this way I came into touch with a copy, but this was lent and re-lent, and finally became impossible to trace. There are some collections of notes of laymen who were set some of these kōans at Kamakura temples, but the teachers when they gave one did not say what number it was, and so in these notes the kōans are not tabulated. It was only after finding a list of contents in one of the Kenchōji manuscripts that I was able to determine the order of the full hundred kōans as recorded in the present work. In Kamakura Zen there were thirty other kōans used mainly by teachers of the ōryū line (mostly at Jufukuji, Zenkōji, and Manjuji – temples traditionally connected with Eisai), which are from Bukedōshinshū (thirteenth volume at Zenkōji), Bushōsōdan (eleventh volume at Jufukuji), and Sōrinzakki (fifteenth volume at Kenchōji), but I have omitted these and present here only the hundred koans of Shōnankattōroku.

Zen tests (sassho) differ with the teacher. Those given to those trained at Enkakuji in the Sōryūkutsu (blue dragon cave) interview room of Master Kōsen (one of the greatest Meiji rōshis) were exceptional tests, and again the tests set by Shunō of Nanzenji, and the formidable Sekisōken tests were not the same. The teachers Keichū and Shinjō had tests of their own. The sassho included here have been taken from a collection of 460 Kamakura sassho recorded in the

Tesshiroku (fourth volume in the manuscript copy). These of course have themselves been picked out from many different interviews with different pupils, but I believe they would have been tests devised by teachers when each kōan was first being set as such; so the collection will have come from something over a hundred different teachers. Of course sometimes a single teacher devised more than one kōan, but if we reckon that Kamakura teachers made 150 kōans, we can take it that the sassho tests devised at the initiation of the separate kōans would have come from over 100 teachers.

The Shōnankattōroku kōans had sermons and discourses with them as well as a note as to the origination of each one, but here only this last is included. The discourses and sermons are so full of old Kamakura words and expressions that annotations would come to be as long as the original text.

Some tests required a 'comment' (chakugo or jakugo). In general these are kept secret and not to be disclosed, but as an example I have included some of the comments on the Mirror Zen poems used at Tōkeiji.

At the end of the sixteenth century Kamakura Zen was gradually deteriorating, and when with the Tokugawa era the country entered a long period of peace, warriors were no longer required to confront the issue of life and death on the battlefield. And it was perhaps for this reason that the quality of those who entered Kamakura Zen was not heroic like that of the old warriors, and both priests and lay followers became fewer. Kamakura Zen begins with 'one word' and ends with absorption in 'one Katzu!' Its main kōan is the Katzu! and unless one could display Zen action at the turning-point of life and death, he was not passed through.

Sometimes a naked sword was at the centre of the interview (in later centuries represented by a fan).

Kamakura Zen was for those who might be called upon to die at any moment, and both teacher and pupils had to have tremendous spirit. Today those who with their feeble power of meditation, casually entertain visions of passing through many kōans, cannot undertake it. In that Zen there were those who spent over ten long years to pass one single kōan (for instance Tsuchiya Daian or Matsui Ryōzen); how many years of painful struggle those like Kidō took to pass through the 'one word' kōans of Kamakura Zen! These days people seem to expect to pass through dozens of kōans in a year, and it cannot be called the same thing at all. Perhaps it might seem pointless to bring out this text now. After the passing of Master Shinjō, there are no more teachers who use Kamakura Zen kōans in their interviews, and again laymen who have actually come under the hammer of this Zen now number only nine, all of them in their seventies or eighties. It is to prevent it falling into untimely oblivion that I bring out this work, so that the fragments which Shunpō Rōshi left shall not be entirely wasted.

The old manuscripts stocked since 1919 in the Dōkai-in repository of Kenchōji were taken out and aired on 1 September 1924, and in the great earthquake more than half of them were destroyed. The records of warrior Zen in particular, held under the collapsed building, became drenched with rainwater and entirely ruined. Thus it has become impossible to make a critical collation of the records, but fortunately from the hundreds of extracts already made, and annotated over many years, it has been possible to investigate

Kamakura Zen and to bring out this collection of a hundred kōans properly edited. Some of the detail had to be determined by comparing as well as possible with what remained of the documents ruined by the earthquake, referring back also to the very many notes which I had myself taken earlier.

Since the earthquake, I have lived the Zen life, for a time in a retreat in Kyūshū, and now buried in my books at Sōfukuji temple. What remained from the earthquake has had to be left. But with my old sick body, it has been impossible to complete the full study of Kamakura Zen quickly, so first of all the full text of just the Shōnankattōroku is to be brought out.

In the autumn of 1919 1 received from Mr Nakayama Takahisa (Ikkan) all the notes about warrior Zen left by the late Shunpō, rōshi of Daitokuji, and to help me with these I examined the old records in the repositories of the Kamakura temples. At that time thanks to the kindness of the kanchō of Kenchōji, the old records of the Donge room were moved to the study in my lodgings there, so that I was able to examine the records of Zen of old masters of many different periods. Again I must express gratitude for the co-operation of Zen master Kananawa, head of the sect administration, thanks to which my examination of documents and records from their stock of rare manuscripts was made so fruitful. Also I was permitted by the priests in charge to go over the records preserved in the repositories at Jufuku, Butsunichi, Garyū and Hōju temples, which provided some precious material on old Zen.

Now by good fortune the manuscript of Shōnankattōroku is ready for publication, and I wish to set down my deepest gratitude and appreciation in regard to all these who have helped so much in the task.

Imai Fukuzan
Spring 1935

2.   Imai Fukuzan's introduction to warrior Zen

According to the Nyūdōsanzenki (Records of Lay Zen) – the postscript of the first volume of the manuscript of Zenkō and the introduction to volume eight of the Kenchō manuscripts – the Zen training of warriors at Kamakura fell into two stages. Up to the end of the Muromachi period (1573), incidents from the training of the early warrior disciples were set as kōans to beginners, and only afterwards were the classical kōans concerning Buddhas and patriarchs used extensively. The incidents from the Zen training of warriors were the kind recorded in the Shōnankattōroku.

But after the end of the Muromachi era, it became common among teachers to present warriors with nothing but classical kōans from the very beginning, and those who used the incidents from warrior training as kōans gradually became very few. So that the three hundred odd kōans of warrior Zen which are known to have existed in Kamakura Zen came to be forgotten.

Among the teachers after Hakuin (died 1768 at age of eighty-four) there were still some who presented these incidents to pupils, but they were not set as kōans to be wrestled with and answered in interviews with the teacher. There were some who, when a pupil stuck too long over one of the classical kōans, brought out one of these old stories of the early samurai as a means to get him round the obstacle and bring him on to the right path from a new direction. In the interviews given by teachers of the Hakuin line, it can be said that no more than twelve or thirteen of the incidents from the training of warriors were known. Only in the Sōryūkutsu (blue dragon cave) line were there still over a score of them in use.

However, teachers of the line from Kogetsu (died in 1751 aged eighty-five; founder of Fukujuji in Kurume, Kyūshū) had a great deal to do with samurai, and in their interviews they preserved a tradition of this Zen, as suited to the inclination of their pupils. They used over a hundred such kōans. The Sōrinzakki (Zen Analects) and Bukedōshinshū (Records of Warriors Aspiring to the Way) list three hundred warrior kōans, but in the Kogetsu tradition one who could pass through seventy-two of them was reckoned to have a complete mastery of the whole three hundred. In the interviews only 108 were being actually set as kōans, and to solve the seventy-two main ones was to pass the whole collection. After the Meiji Restoration (1868) the last teachers to use them were Shinjō of the Hakuin line, and Shunō of the Kogetsu line, and there were none who followed them in this, so that at present (1920) there are no teachers who use them. Thus there are very few today who know anything about the incidents recorded in the Nyūdōsanzenki and the other collections.

By the end of Muromachi the Kamakura kōans were gradually being forgotten, and in the Zen which followed Hakuin they were almost entirely discarded. There was however still some tradition about them in Kyūshū, and at the time of the Meiji Restoration Zen teachers all over the country were continually being asked about this Zen by samurai of the main Kyūshū clans like Satsuma and Chōshū. Many Rinzai teachers found they could not answer. However in the Sōtō line, Ekidō the abbot of Sōjiji temple, Kankei the abbot of Eiheiji, Bokusan of Kasuisai, and others knew warrior Zen well, and could meet the questions of the Kyūshū civilians and warriors.

In the Rinzai line, there was an impression that samurai Zen had been Zen of repeating the Name of Amida (nembutsu Zen), and the teachers did not know about the Kamakura kōans. Gyokai, abbot of Zōjōji, of the Jōdo sect, and Tetsujō, abbot of Chionin, and other spiritual leaders of this line taught samurai Zen as being Nembutsu, and often preached to the high officials and generals of those times. The teachers of other lines knew the stories, but simply related them and did not set them as kōans to be wrestled with. And in fact what goes on in the interview room is different with each line, and is not something that ought to be lightly spoken about.

Warrior Zen began with the samurai who came to Eisai at Jufukuji in Kamakura, from 1215. (This temple was burnt down in 1247 and again in 1395, many of the records being lost.) Historically this Zen was taught in the interviews of Rinzai masters, but now there are few within the Rinzai lines who know of it, though quite some outside who have some knowledge. This is an ironic fact, on discovering which many inquirers into Zen have had to suppress a smile.

In the first years of Meiji, the Daikyō-in in Tokyo began work examining old records in Zen temples, collaborating with some priests of the Rinzai line as well. (The Daikyō-in was set up with some official support to advise on religious matters.) A glance at their bulletin makes the facts clear. Temples all over the country sent old records concerning warrior Zen to the Daikyō-in for examination. The material was there classified under five heads: Zen connected with the Imperial palace, with the Shōgun rulers, with nobles, with the gentry of various clans, and with simple warriors. Those parts which recorded kōans were collated. This project was initiated at the suggestion of a monk named Taikōan. It was found that the Rinzai temples, obsessed with the principle 'no setting up of words', had not merely seen little necessity to keep records, but were very indifferent to the preservation of what records did exist. So there is very little material about what kōans the teachers gave to the princes, to the nobles, to the warriors and to the ordinary people. Again, one incident which takes up five or six pages in records of the Sōtō and Ōbaku Zen lines, in the Rinzai account may have barely half a page, so that sometimes it is quite difficult to make out all the main points. There are those who maintain that this is in accordance with the principle of directness, that 'just one inch of the blade kills the man', but if this principle is applied to historical records, along with the other one of not setting up words in the first place, surely it is going too far.

Parts of the Daikyō-in records have been damaged by insects and so on, but what follows is a list of the published collections of records which were then available to them.

The *Hōmeishū* (Record of the cry of the phoenix – in the records of Kenninji) and the *Undaigendan* (Discourses from the cloud dais – records of Nanzenji) in reporting the same incidents differ only in the length and detail of their accounts. Both of them begin with the interviews between the Empress Tachibana (Danrin), consort of Emperor Saga, and the Chinese Zen master Gikū, about AD 815, and follow with an account of the interest taken in Zen by sixteen emperors, from Gotoba (1183–98) up to Go-mizuno-o (1611–29). Both of them have the imperial utterances expressed in classical Yamatokotoba, which are thus difficult to read without a translation into standard language. For this reason Shunpō himself had the impression that these are paraphrases of old Court documents. However a copy in possession of Ekidō of Sōjiji was finally discovered which turned out to have these sections all transcribed into orthodox Chinese characters and thus easy to read.

Sōrinzakki (Zen analects) and a commentary on it were pieced together by Shunpō from various copies of parts of it which existed in the Kyōto temples, though owing to the fragmentary nature of the material he was never able to reconstruct a complete original text. In any case none of the Kyōto copies have anything before ōnin (1467) and they stop at Genroku (1688), so that they cannot be compared with the detailed historical accounts in the Kamakura records. The most complete version of the Sōrinzakki and its commentary existed in Zenkōji in Kamakura, but even this goes no further than 1716 and can tell us nothing after that.

Bukedōshinshū (Records of warriors aspiring to the Way – no connection at all with the published book of the same name) is a collection of biographies of warriors who entered Zen training, took interviews with a teacher for some years, and were given a Zen name by the teacher when they had mastered the principle of Zen.

Bushōsōdan (Zen stories of warriors and generals) and Ryueizenna (Zen tales of willow camp) give accounts of Zen incidents from the lives of generals from Hōjō Tokiyori up to the Tokugawas. In the Jufukuji library these two have been bound together as an appendix to the Bukedōshinshū, with the title Bumontetsuganzei (pupil of the warrior eye). This was written out by priest Gettei of the Jufukuji sub-temple Keikōan.

Nyūdōsanzenki (Accounts of lay Zen) and Gosannyūdōshū (Lay training at Rinzai temples) are accounts of warriors training at the five temples of Kamakura.

Shōnankattōroku (Record of Kamakura kōans) has a hundred kōans consisting of incidents from the training of warriors. A full account of this book is given in the other appendix.

Ka-an-zatsuroku (Analects of Ka-an) is a random collection of notes of incidents concerning the warriors, nobles and officials who came from all over the country to priest Ka-an at Manjuji. At the beginning of the Meiji era many temples had manuscript copies of this, but now (1920) there is only one copy, consisting of twelve fascicules copied by Sōkū of Hōkokuji.

Zendōguzūki (Record of the propagation of Zen) begins with the meeting at Jufukuji between Eisai and Gyōyū, and gives further accounts of Zen training in Rinzai temples up to Ō-ei (1394). There is a manuscript copy in the library at Nirayama.

Zenjōmonshōkan (Mirror of Zen samādhi) consists of biographies of warriors who trained under Zen teachers and finally received the full 'approval' (inka) from them. This book extracts from the accounts in Bukedōshinshū, Gosannyūdōshū and others those cases where the master finally gave approval to the pupil as having completed the training.

This book was at Kanazawa before the partial dispersal of the library there, and is known to bibliophiles as an 'ex-Kanazawa book' as in the case also of Shōinmanpitsu (Jottings from the shade of the banana tree), Zenrinrōeishū (Zen songs of retainers), Shōchōshū (Pine and sea), Towafūsōshū (Wind and seaweed of eastern Japan), Sekirozakki (Jottings from a stone hearth), Shōtōseigo (Holy words from pine and tide), Fukugenrenpeki (Wall round the fount of bliss), Hamanomezarashi (Vision of the beach), Hanagakishū (Flowering hedge anthology), and others. All these record incidents of the warrior Zen tradition, and also some of them give poems which the warriors composed as answers to the kōan tests. (This kind of answer is technically called agyo.)

In 1400 Zen master Taigaku Shūei made an examination of the Kanazawa library and catalogued the Zen manuscripts. Later Zenju, the 178th Master of Kenchōji, when he became the teacher at Ashikaga college, examined the old manuscripts at the Kanazawa and Nirayama libraries, and catalogued many hundreds of the old Zen records which he found there. The Zen teachers who were members of Daikyō-in, in their search for accounts of warrior Zen, found and borrowed for examination, through the librarian Suzuki Sōei, many of the old manuscripts there. The examination made it clear that the kōans about which officials and warriors at the beginning of the Meiji era were asking Rinzai teachers, were in fact very early incidents of the training of warriors by teachers of this same Rinzai sect.

No one can estimate how many hundreds and thousands of lay people have practised Zen in Japan since the Empress

Danrin at the beginning of the ninth century, and there must have been innumerable records of the kōans set to them. The first time I saw any material on warrior Zen was in 1872 or 73, when Zen master Bokusan presented my father with a notebook made by the Sōtō master Gattan, and a manuscript written by Zuiun of the Ōbaku sect. From these I got some idea of how teachers of Sōtō and Ōbaku used to handle their warrior pupils in the past. Then after attending the addresses in Tokyo given by Shunpō, rōshi of Daitokuji, about the old records like Bushōsōdan and Bukedōshinshū, I discovered the still more drastic means which were used in the Rinzai sect for warriors. Later, Bairyō, kanchō of Nanzenji, gave me copies of Undaigendan, Hōmeishū and other texts, from which I came to know about the direct Zen traditions which there had been at the Imperial palace. Only after seeing the Shōnankattōroku text which Yamaoka Tesshū had received from Shōjō of Ryūtaku temple in Izu, did I first come to know that there had been a separate Zen tradition at Kamakura.

In 1872, Master Tekisui was elected general head to represent the three Zen sects, and there were many laymen training in Zen. Master Shunpō too was active in the Daikyō-in, and many leading figures in Zen were studying warrior Zen traditions; material about it was being collected in Tokyo so that there were good opportunities to study the kōans of that tradition. But as in the case of the Hōmeishū text, where the Imperial utterances in the palace tradition were reported in Yamatokotoba, here too there was much use of classical Japanese words of antiquity, which could not be understood without a gloss in contemporary Japanese. In the Kamakura records again, there are many local words from several centuries previously. To read the records themselves one has to peruse an old manuscript entitled 'Old Deer-brush' by Master Sanpaku (156th Master of Enkakuji), and then one has to know the obsolete words. Furthermore, the founders of all the Kamakura temples were Chinese of the Sung or Yūan dynasties, and in the old accounts there is much Chinese transcribed phonetically in a distorted way by writers who did not understand it. Without the glossary compiled by Ryūha, the 178th Master of Kenchōji, there are many passages which could hardly be read, let alone understood. In an old Zenkōji record (which was still preserved in Jufukuji around 1868) there is a report of a meeting between Hōjō Tokimune and Bukkō Kokushi, and in it comes this: 'Kun-sun-rii, kun-sun-rii, raunau, ya-shi-yan-kin-gu-a'. Today there is hardly a soul who could read this and understand it. It was always supposed that it must have been some kōan. Round about 1875, when there were many great figures in Zen coming and going round the Daikyō-in, there was no one, not even Shunpō Rōshi who was consultant professor to the three head temples Daitokuji, Myōshinji and Kenninji, who could suggest any meaning for this Sung Chinese which Bukkō spoke to Tokimune. Nobody had any idea what it was. But when the glossary by Ryūha was acquired by the Daikyō-in, the passage kun-sun-rii ... turned out surprisingly to be 'Come in, come in! I have something to say to Your Honour.' This caused general laughter. In the Kamakura temples there are many similar old records of Sung Chinese transcribed phonetically. So there are many inconveniences in the study of warrior Zen there. But after being presented with the Reikenroku (Record of the spiritual sword – the copy in the Butsunichi-an is called Jintōroku) with the red-ink notes by Kaigan Rōshi and textual amendments by Tōkoku Rōshi, I found that the bulk of the 500 warrior kōans recorded in the Sōrinzakki and elsewhere were Kamakura Zen.

For his research on old Kamakura Zen, Shunpō made many notes on the backs of used pieces of paper. (He almost never used a clean sheet, but always the backs of pieces of wrapping paper and so on. The only time he used a new sheet of paper was for a final fair copy.) Before he could collate all his material into a text, he had to return to Kyōto in 1875, on account of urgent affairs connected with the administration of the colleges attached to the great temples there – so I heard indirectly from others. No one else who had been studying warrior Zen had completed any of the drafts either, and finally it was left to the general research council of ten Zen temples (I recall that this was founded in 1875), which entrusted it to Imagita Kōsen Rōshi. At that time however he was himself engaged in many projects, and from Enkakuji was promoting Zen vigorously in the Kantō area. He became head of the seven lines of the Rinzai sect, and with all his administrative engagements had no time for examining ancient records. He therefore divided the task among the many laymen who were training under him.

Ichinyo (Miyata Chūyū), Ryūmon (Hirata Yasumaru) and others examined the records of Zen at the palace; Mumon (Oi Kiyomichi), Rakuzan (Suzuki Yoshitaka) and others took the documents on shōgun Zen; Ryōzen (Ishii Tokihisa), Katei (Yamada Toshiaki) and others studied warrior Zen; Daian and Kido worked solely on Kamakura Zen. But many of them had official duties and little time for the research, and if thev were sent abroad it had to be set aside. Moreover those officials in the ministries of Education and the Army who had given support round about 1878, were completely occupied with their political responsibilities when the Satsuma rebellion broke out, and had no opportunity for anything else. Senior men like ōtori Keisuke and Soejima had to carry out diplomatic missions abroad, and the interest in warrior Zen slipped into the background.

After the death of Yamaoka Tesshū in 1889, those who could say anything on this kind of Zen gradually became few; Katsu Kaishū, Takahashi Deishū, Shimao Tokuan and other great Zen laymen died, and almost no one knew anything about the subject. While the Daikyō-in existed in Tokyo there were a good many among the Zen teachers who knew about this laymen's Zen, and there were many who used Zen stories of the warriors. As we can see from their recorded sermons, Masters Dokuon and Keichū were speaking on palace Zen, Mugaku, Teizan and Shunpō on warrior Zen in general, and Kōsen and Shinjo on Kamakura Zen in particular. But as there was nobody who could present Kamakura Zen apart from the dozen kōans which were given in interviews, teachers who had not seen texts like the Sōrinzakki and its commentary tended to think that Kamakura Zen was nothing more than these dozen kōans – perhaps to the quiet amusement of men like Tesshū and Kaishū. But Shunpō Rōshi on the other hand had heard the discourses of Master Myōhō of Hofukuji (at Iyama in Bicchū) on the Bukedōshinshū, Reikenroku, Bushōsōdan and so on, and knew well about the Kamakura kōans, information which he transmitted to inquirers in Tokyo; those who wanted warrior Zen called him prince of teachers.

In 1875 he left Tokyo and in March two years later passed away in Kyōto. It is just fifty years since his death, and there are left in Tokyo only nine people who came into touch with his greatness, all of them fine vigorous old men. Talking to them about the teacher and about Kamakura Zen, one has the strong feeling of how Zen has changed. For the fiftieth anniversary in March this year, Zen master Nyoishitsu of Sōfukuji desires to distribute some work of Shunpō as a 'fan for the eternal breeze of the Way'. But the only draft which the teacher left was one called Shōkaigifu (Voyager on the ocean of the absolute), which was not concerned with warrior Zen, and all the rest was no more than notes not yet written up into a text.

When I looked through these notes and fragments formerly, I noticed that a great number were concerned with Kamakura Zen; but to arrange these miscellaneous scraps written on the backs of used pieces of paper into a connected text was not something that could be done in a hurry. It would have been impossible, with the limitations imposed by the publication plan, to write up everything connected with Kamakura Zen. So it came about that Master Nyoishitsu began to press for the publication, on the fiftieth anniversary, of a first part only. This was to be an edited and supplemented edition of the Shōnankattōroku.

The whole work projected is to be called Bushizenkienshū (Records of warrior Zen training) and the present text is to be just a first part. I have been told that there are in existence 5,600 pages about warrior Zen, bound into thirty-six volumes of a hundred pages each, which have been produced by laymen under the direction of great Zen teachers. And I have wondered whether it might be possible to put them into permanent form. With the loss of so many of the old manuscripts in the Kantō earthquake, it is not feasible to collect and collate all the material in a short time. All I can hope is, that one day I shall complete the work on warrior Zen, of which this Shōnankattōroku is to be the first part. I am a retired scholar already over seventy, and writing is more and more a burden. But I have a dharma-link with my old teacher Shunpō, whose discourses I so often attended, and I rejoice that the draft of the work has been completed for publication on the fiftieth anniversary of his passing. I beg the indulgence of readers for faults they may find in it.

Imai Fukuzan
1925

3. Index of names and technical terms

This index gives the Chinese characters for less familiar names and technical terms in the previous two appendices. Well-known names such as Bukkō and terms such as kōan are omitted. In some cases, Imai has indicated an unusual reading, and these readings are followed here. Some of the characters are rare and have had to be written by hand.

下	語				AGYO
梅	嶺				BAIRYŌ
穆	山				BOKUSAN
武	家	道	心	集	BUKEDŌSHINSHŪ
武	門	鐵	眼	晴	BUMONTETSUGANZEI
武	將	叢	談		BUSHŌSŌDAN
佛	日	菴			BUTSUNICHIAN
大	安				DAIAN
大	永				DAIEI
大	教	院			DAIKYŌIN
檀	林				DANRIN
泥	舟				DEISHŪ
同	契	院			DOKAIIN
獨	園				DOKUON

曇華	DONGE
道友摠持	DŌYŪ SŌJI
奕堂	EKIDŌ
福源聯壁	FUKUGEN RENPEKI
福山	FUKUZAN
月江	GAKKŌ
臥龍	GARYŪ
月潭	GATTAN
月庭	GATTEI
義空	GIKŪ
義翁	GIŌ
五山入道集	GŌSANNYŪDŌSHŪ
鼇巓	GŌTEN
行誠	GYŌKAI
行勇	GYŌYŪ
濱のめざらし	HAMA-NO-MEZARASHI
寶福寺	HŌFUKUJI
寶珠	HŌJU
鳳鳴集	HŌMEISHŪ
一如	ICHINYO
一貫	IKKAN
寂菴	JAKUAN
壽福寺	JUFUKUJI
可菴雜錄	KAANZATSUROKU

花垣集　KAENSHŪ

海舟　KAISHŪ

環溪　KANKEI

可睡齊　KASUISAI

華亭　KATEI

敬沖　KEICHŪ

桂光奄　KEIKŌAN

虚道　KIDŌ

機緣　KIEN

古月　KOGETSU

孤峰　KOHŌ

金剛圈　KONGŌKEN

洪川　KŌSEN

敎乘禪　KYŌJŌZEN

萬壽寺　MANJUJI

明月院　MEIGETSUIN

無學　MUGAKU

無隱　MUIN

無門　MUMON

妙峰　MYŌHŌ

明應　MYŌŌ

如意室　NYOISHITSU

入道参禪記　NYŪDŌSANZENKI

黄龍　ŌRYŪ

太岳周榮	ŌTAKE SHŪEI
來迎院	RAIGOIN
樂山	RAKUZAN
蘭山秘記	RANZANHIKI
靈劍錄	REIKENROKU
龍峰	RYŌHŌ
了然	RYŌZEN (RYŌNEN)
柳營禪話	RYUEIZENNA
龍派	RYŪHA
西來	SAIRAI
三伯	SANPAKU
拶抄	SASSHŌ
拶門	SATSUMON
石爐雜記	SEKIROZAKKI
石窓軒	SEKISŌKEN
即今禪	SHIKIN (SOKKON) ZEN
眞淨	SHINJŌ
神刀錄	SHINTŌROKU
松潮集	SHŌCHŌSHŪ
聖一	SHŌICHI
蕉蔭漫筆	SHŌINMANPITSU
星定	SHŌJŌ
松壽醒語	SHŌJUSEIGO
性海艖洴	SHŌKAIGIFU

湘	南	葛	錄			SHŌNANKATTŌROKU
宗	玖					SHŪKU
舜	應					SHUNŌ
峻	峰					SHUNPŌ
叢	林	雑	記			SŌRINZAKKI
蒼	龍	窟				SORYŪKUTSU
祖	山					SOZAN
崇	福	寺				SŌFUKUJI
翠	岩	遺	筆			SUIGANYUIHITSU
退	耕	庵				TAIKŌAN
貞	山					TEIZAN
滴	水					TEKISUI
天	源					TENGEN
鐵	糂	錄				TESSHIROKU
鐵	舟					TESSHŪ
徹	定					TETSUJŌ
桃	菴					TŌAN
東	慶	寺				TŌKEIJI
韜	谷					TŌKOKU
得	庵					TOKUAN
東	倭	風	藻	集		TŌWAFŪSŌSHŪ
雲	臺	玄	談			UNDAIGENDAN
禪	道	弘	通	記		ZENDŌGUZŪKI
禪	珠					ZENJU

禪興寺	ZENKŌJI
禪林朗詠集	ZENRINRŌEISHŪ
藏叟	ZŌSŌ
瑞雲	ZUIUN